*"The language of Spirit is
Transformation."*

JANITH

ON WINGS OF TRUTH

by

JANITH

A Channeled Book

compiled by:

Teri Griswold

illustrations by:

Anabel Maresca

introductions by:

Carol Gino

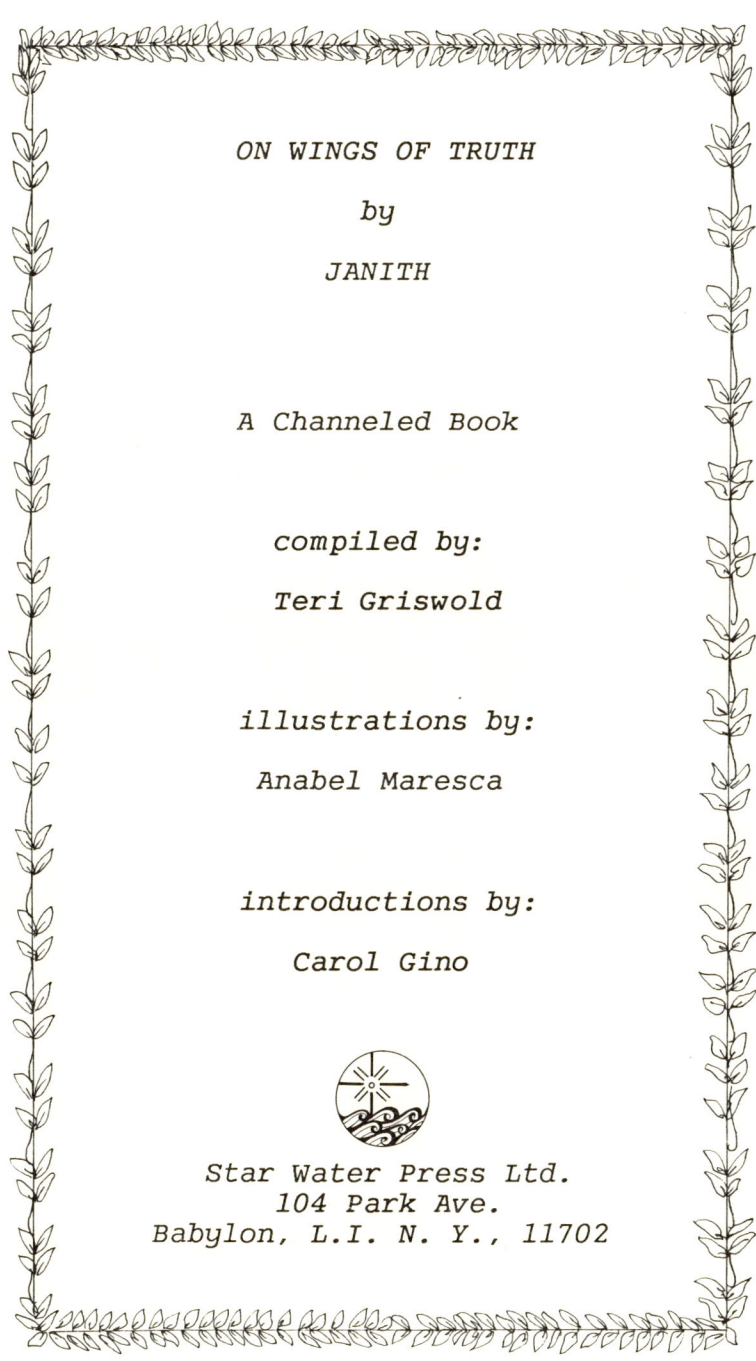

Star Water Press Ltd.
104 Park Ave.
Babylon, L.I. N. Y., 11702

Star Water Press Ltd.
104 Park Ave.
Babylon, L.I. N.Y., 11702

First paperback edition 1987

Manufactured in the United States of America
10 9 8 7 6 5 4 3 2 1

To the Child within each of us

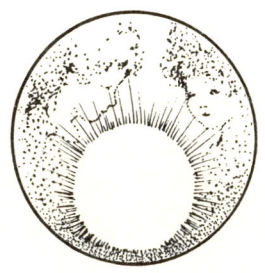

I have known Janith for three years now and I can't imagine life without her. She has brought me insight, laughter and healing and in the time we have been together, she has taken me from skeptic to believer, from half to wholeness, from death to life. With much love, I would like to thank her.

Teri

A SPIRIT SOARS,

A SOUL DISCOVERS.

A SPIRIT IS FREE

A SOUL IS BURDENED

THE DIFFERENCE BETWEEN THEM

IS ONE OF OUR PLANE AND YOURS

IT IS ONE OF WHAT

MUST REMAIN AN

INDIVIDUAL

TO TOUCH DOWN INTO

PHYSICAL BODY.

A SOUL IS A MAN'S SOUL.

WE, AS SPIRITS, DO NOT HAVE A SOUL.

THEREFORE THERE IS,

AS YOU WOULD LIKE TO SAY

A SILVER CORD

NOT ONLY BETWEEN

SOUL AND PHYSICAL BODY,

BUT BETWEEN

PHYSICAL BODY, SOUL AND SPIRIT.

 *INTRODUCTION*

I grew up on fantastic myths and rich stories of brave heroes who were tested by Olympian gods; heroes who proved their courage and sincerity by undertaking incredible voyages and accomplishing impossible deeds and who always won. Good always triumphed over evil.

Accordingly, I believed my world had been created by a loving and omnipotent personal God who provided that each of his children be constantly attended and protected by his or her own special guardian angel.

Each night as my father tucked me in to bed, he fed me more rich myth to grow on. And each day with my completely balanced meals, my mother fed me more "reality."

I went to Catholic school where the nuns were mostly kind, though their idea of God was far more punishing than the One I knew in my heart. Here, my dreams were fed even more by the stories of visions and apparitions visited upon the very good and the very young.

The constant prayer in my heart while I kneeled in church and my lips moved to the "Our Father" or the "Hail Mary" was, "Dear God...If a kid like Bernadette got a vision of Our Lady, why can't I have one?" Bernadette was, as far as I was concerned, just another kid who happened to live in Lourdes, and who couldn't have been trying any harder than I to be good. Back then, my religious aspirations were competitive.

Life and time passed and mother's vision of reality seemed closer to the reality I was experiencing than the stories Dad had told. And so as many of us do, a large part of me grew up and traded the vision of my heart for the newer vision of my mind.

This new god, the god of rational mind, was fine when things were going well. I was rewarded in wordly terms; I was successful. Still, I found whenever a major tragedy hit in my life, I immediately resorted to the stronger knowledge of my heart, turned to my guardian angel and hollered help.

I wouldn't pretend to you that I had never lost faith. That would be untrue. And I was no uncomplaining Job. During that entire period of my life when I traded my omnipotent, personal, compassionate God for the god of intellect, rational mind, and science, my God seemed a product of infancy and innocence and I, and most of my friends, gave it up and stopped believing.

Instead, I read, studied and spent my spare time accumulating "facts," hoping somehow to transform all that information into some kind of wisdom.

At the time I had been working in hospitals for years watching and caring for the sick and dying. Medicine became my god. A savage god. And very limited. When I realized that the limitations of science and medicine limited me, I began to search again. I went back to school, got another degree, and then spent several more years reading theology, psychology, and philosophy. Finally, I began to study Eastern philosophy and to read some of the great mystics.

And a funny thing happened. After all those years of searching and serving those false gods, I realized that the fantastic myths and rich stories that my father had told were true. Suddenly, there was a movement called "Transpersonal Psychology" that told of people in the "real" world, the world of here and now, who were taking those heroes journeys into the incredible and unknown.

But it was not until my grandson Gregory died, and when my own child, Teri, desperately needed comfort and answers I couldn't give, that I found the omnipotent and compassionate God of my childhood again. And I realized, that as He had promised, He had sent with each of us a guardian angel.

Teri's was called Janith. First she
appeared in automatic writings and then
when Teri allowed - after a year's trial
of trust and truth - she began to speak
through Teri in words while I recorded
and later transcribed the sessions.

She didn't _appear_ so it couldn't be
called a visitation now, instead it's
called channeling. But Janith, who
describes herself, metaphorically, as
looking much like the Angel Gabriel,
helped to heal not only me and my child
but many others as well. In the New Age,
she doesn't call herself an angel, she
refers to herself as "The Spirit of
Creative Communications from the Core
Group of Healers that are closest to the
Thirteenth Master." But I know, both in
my heart and in my mind, that she's an
angel and that The Thirteenth Master is
the compassionate, omnipotent, loving God
of my childhood.

Because there are so many discarnate
entities coming through now and speaking,
Janith wants to provide a balance, to
provide a true base of spirituality. She
wants to give some guidelines to "human
livings" to help them discern the truth
from the untruths that are being spoken
now.

When I asked her how we could
distinguish between the quality and
validity of these spirits or disembodied
entities, she answered in this way.

"Human minds, human souls, are capable of good judgement. They are capable of interpreting the spiritual on not only an instinctual level, an intuitive level but also on a rational level. I feel it is quite important to look with your mind, not only your mind's eye, at these answers, at these communications. Are they causing harm? Do they interrupt with destiny? Are they taking from more than they are giving to? Basically, it is much the same as a very good human relationship, a very giving relationship, a very comfortable relationship. Also, is it a growing relationship? This must remain the most important test, if you will, of a channel spirit communication relationship. For if it does not allow or precipitate growth, then it is and does become the worst form of stagnation."

Teri, Janith and I would like to share with you what we know to be "reality." It's an expanded view, one that shows spirit as loving, helpful, comforting, practical....and funny.

We offer it to you, on Janith's suggestion, in order to build a bridge in this New Age between "human livings" and spirit, in the hope that shared knowledge between two worlds can help to hasten our evolution toward a brighter tomorrow.

Janith

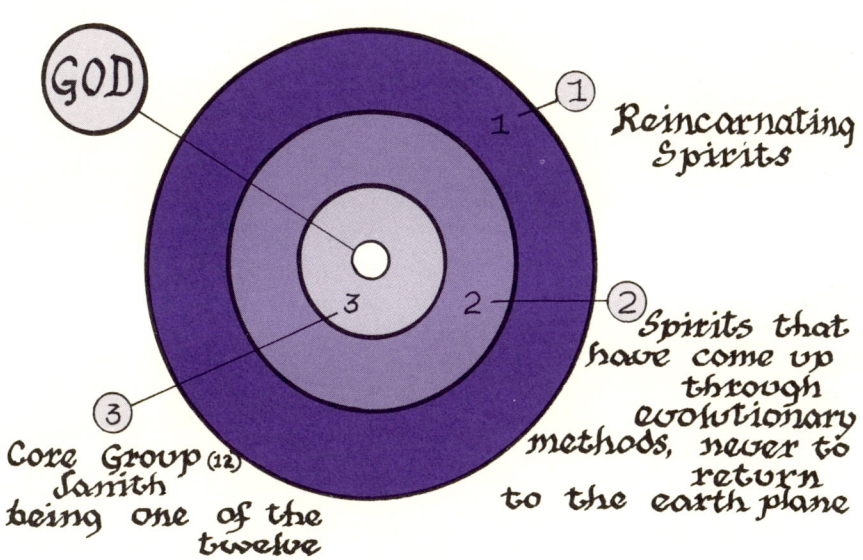

GOD

1 — Reincarnating Spirits

2 — Spirits that have come up through evolutionary methods, never to return to the earth plane

3 — Core Group (12) Janith being one of the twelve

CORE GROUP

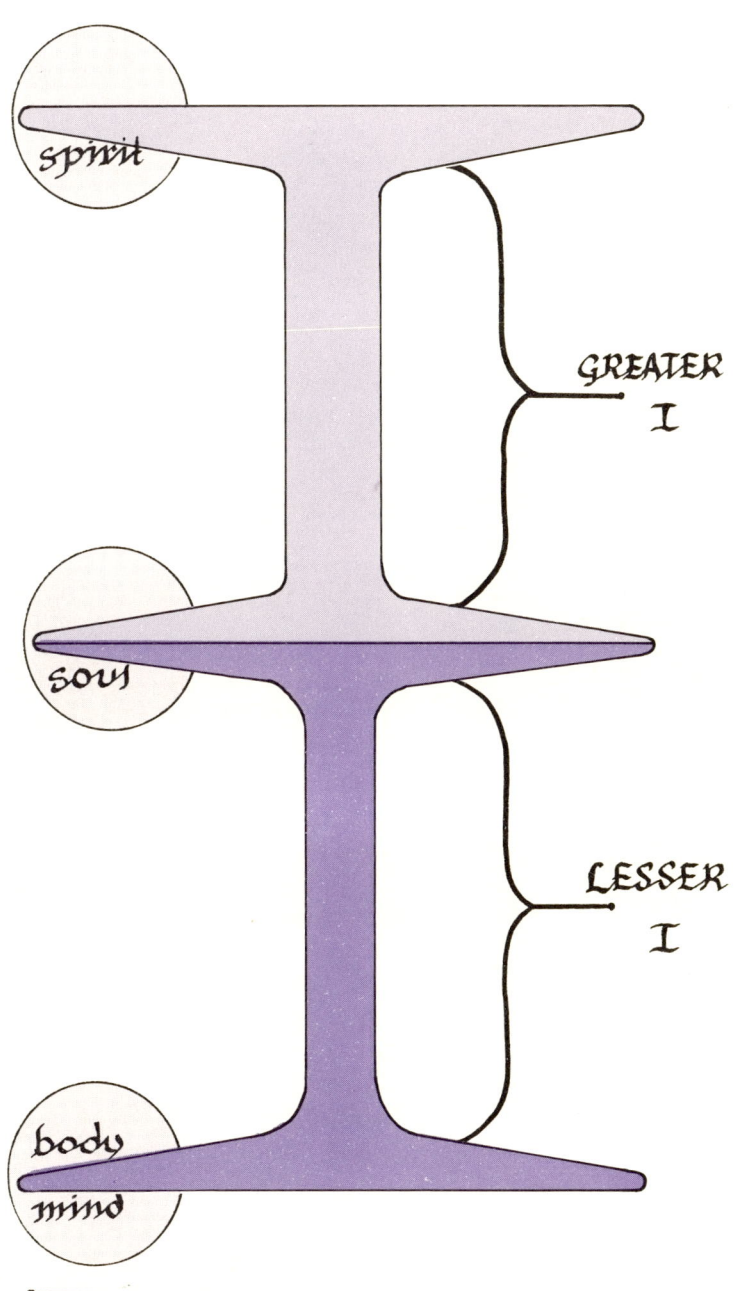

GREATER ~ LESSER I

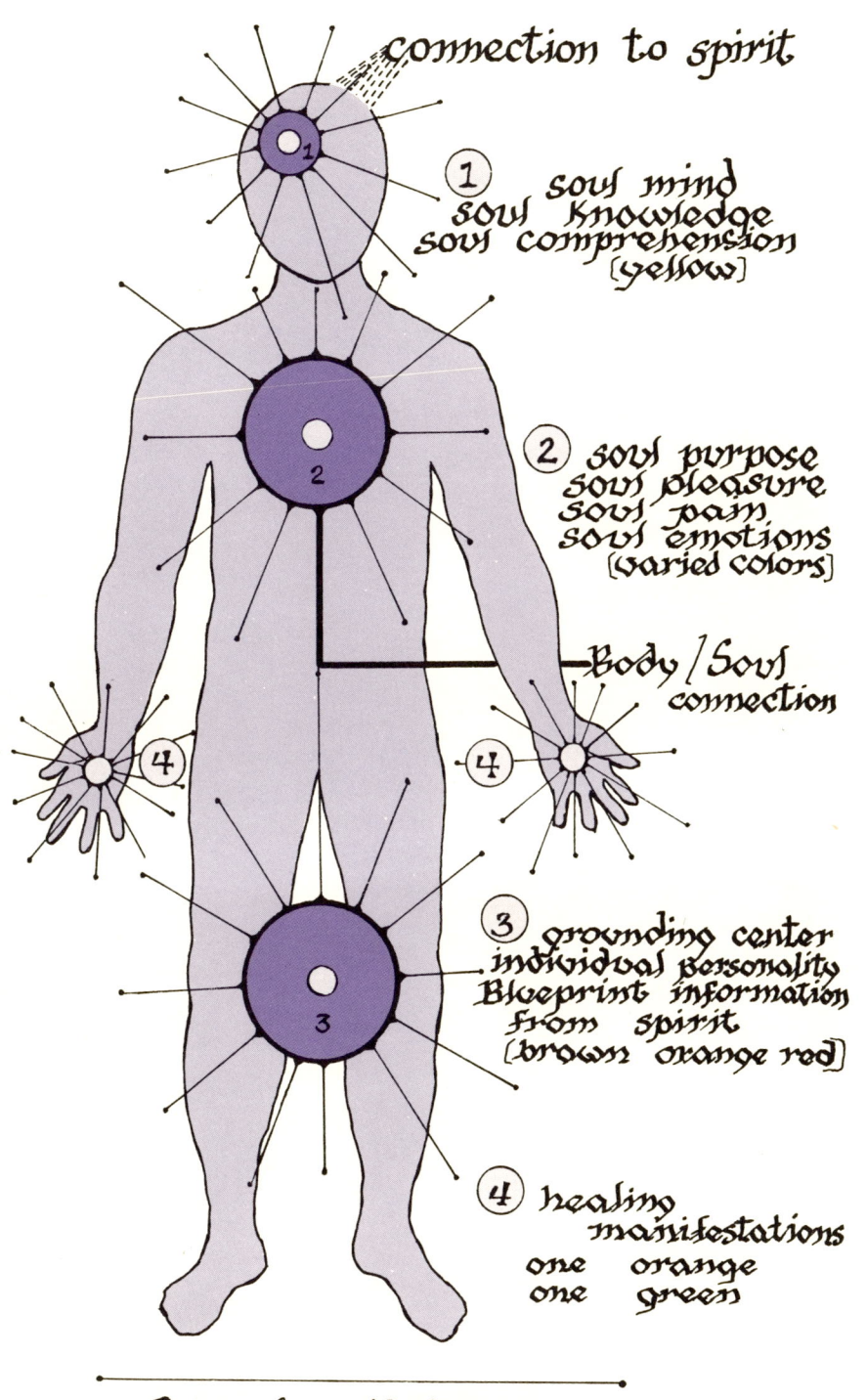

connection to spirit

1. soul mind
   soul knowledge
   soul comprehension
   (yellow)

2. soul purpose
   soul pleasure
   soul pain
   soul emotions
   (varied colors)

Body/Soul connection

3. grounding center
   individual personality
   Blueprint information
   from spirit
   (brown orange red)

4. healing
   manifestations
   one orange
   one green

SOUL BODY

EARTHPOINT PROBLEMS

_"There is a greater cause
than that of the earth's
known purposes. That cause
is to be of a greater mind,
a greater consciousness,
a greater compassion."_

JANITH

Janith's manner is light, her voice is sweet and loving and often there is a sense of compassion for us in her answers that is hard to capture in the written word. Also, often she is very funny. I hope that we've managed to give some of that "sense" of her in these communications. All of them have been transcribed from tapes exactly as they were spoken so that though sentences may not be grammatically correct, the meanings will be clear. Janith suggests that these answers be processed through soul mind, not completely through rational mind, because more information will be gained in that way. If, as was the problem with me, you find you don't know what or where soul mind is, just relax and let the words fall in. There is a place in you that understands more than your mind, and that place will recognize and understand Janith's words.

In trying to organize this material we have decided to use categories, categories that were by necessity arbitrary. A lot of this information is free form so it slips over the edges of any limits we try to impose on it.

The questions we've chosen to place in the first chapter are the answers Janith has given for the "problems" we have on earth at this point in time. These are problems that we struggle to find larger meanings for in our everyday existence, ones that there seem to be no real answers to in our world. They fall loosely into the categories we call current events or ethical and moral issues.

Q - What is Good?   What is Evil?

A - Good is a person's knowledge of his task.   Good is God, The One, The Light. Good is never evil, never malicious. Good are you.   Good is our understanding and communicating.   Good is the trees, flowers and bees.   Good is understanding and receiving help when you need it. Good is all.

Bad is one's ignorance of the Light. Bad is one's unacceptance of a life plan once made.   Growth is good and bad stunts growth.   This constitutes evil.

Q - Is Truth or Good ultimately right? And which should be the focus in one's life?

A - Truth is good, and good, truth. Ultimate Truth not subtle truth.   Which do you speak of?   Subtle truth should be used with discretion.   This kind of truth can be used to hurt, to maim another and can be no good.   Ultimate Truth is one of All - Knowledge and only good springs from such a source.   Why did you not ask of Love?   Is that not an ultimate goal in your own outward eyes?

Good is a strived for goal.   But if one of these must be more pronounced than the other, it should always be Truth, ultimate in nature.   Otherwise good will not fall from a source.   This is good.

Q - What about Love?

A - Love must remain the ultimate in power in striving for Truth, in living the good. Love for thyself, love for thy friend, love for thy children - and other ones close in relation.

Love for thy enemy may become the most important - for once an enemy is truly loved on a soul level of each; not only an outward level, then my children, no enemies will be found in your world. Knowledge of the Light can be a beginning step toward the love that must come to your plane.

Love is the connection of souls. Love is the meaning behind the Light. Love is the basis of our existence. A true love of spirit is what is required of humans, especially humans in the service areas of life.

Q - Are there different types of Love?

A - Of course. Love that a man feels for a woman. This type of love, unless they have traveled many lives together, does not run as deep as soul love which is the second type of love. Soul love is one of divine trust in knowledge of the Light, God, the One, of us and you, of all there is. And then there is mother - child love that runs closer to soul love than does woman - man love unless as we have spoken before of many lives and many times these two have shared.

Q - Is cause and effect the basis of our society's belief system?

A - There is a basic cause and effect that your society believes in. Yet, that cause always seems to be themselves and the effect always seems to be a direct reaction of themselves. That is not really the way cause and effect should work.

Q - Do you wish to tell us how cause and effect should work?

A - There is a greater cause than that of the individual. There is a greater cause than that of the earth's known purposes. That cause is to be of a greater consciousness, a greater mind, a greater compassion. The effect would then become the ultimate enlightening experience which all would achieve if the cause could be recognized.

Q - What do you feel the sexual revolution and the women's movement was and is about?

A - It is about finding the balance between the masculine energies and the feminine energies, and a balancing on the earth plane.

Q - Do you think it's a good thing?

A - Balance is always a good thing.

Q - Is it right to sustain life beyond its natural time with life support systems?

A - Life support systems are good for those who haven't finished their work here. It gives them more time. Even time in coma is good when needed. The mind, soul/spirit, and emotions are still taking their course.

If a child is put on a respirator and it's his or her time to go, don't worry. They will leave their body when it's time. They get very good at astral and decide when it's time to go. Then, after, the body will die.

Put on respirators who you must. Always God, the One, The All - Knowledge is the judge of when one's life plan is over and will speak to the higher self of that individual. And all shall be right. It is intended for good, of this we have no complaint.

Q - Is Euthanasia ever right?

A - Killing is not right no matter where or when. The soul has already entered such human livings and then a soul is taken before it's time to surrender. Sad that human livings do not look for other answers. Limited is their understanding of concepts. We hope their concepts of Life, Death, and us may be changed through some of our communications.

Q - Is there a difference, Janith, between Euthanasia and organ harvesting?

A - What kind of difference?

Q - You said Euthanasia is never right. Organ harvesting seems to take the organs...

A - Another problem with this world that you live in is that people always try to take what is not theirs to take. This is never good - for where is the balance?

Q - Why do so many people seem to have trouble donating organs for transplants?

A - Once they recognize that the body is not their own, they will know they have no claim on it, so it is not something that they can donate for it is not theirs. If the idea is that it is yours, then you have a right to say no. If the idea is one of no possession, then that becomes a reality and it is taken easily for it is no one's.

Q - When one has a terminal illness is it cosmically right to kill oneself before the complete deterioration of body and mind?

A - One will not be <u>able</u> to kill oneself if it is not time.

Q - To what extent am I my brother's keeper? How can we know when not to interfere?

A - We are all our brother's keeper but not a caging keeper, a freeing keeper. As long as this is kept in mind, good is being done, truth is being let out, and love is overflowing onto others and the earth.

Q - How do we know when our helping begins to harm another?

A - Do not become a caging keeper of your brothers - other human livings. For this is when harm is done to another's growth process. All is well as long as you are a freeing keeper, a loving helper. And remember, Life is the greatest teacher. All that one may do is help and guide, not teach.
Also, remember not to take on another's learning process for this also stops the growth process. As long as one is aiding in the growth process, one is helping. When one sees growth being stunted, that is when to end this helper affair.

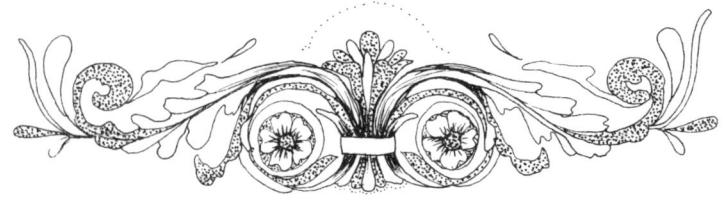

Q - Is intent or action the determining factor in deciding whether something is good or bad?

A - Why must you ones always separate one from the other? This cannot be the case. For if it were, intentions would be all we would live by. One must have intention enforced by action.

Do you know that one man sat on his stone and intended to get up to eat something so he would not starve? Four years later he awoke, still not fed, and on another plane.

Action is the completion of intent. There cannot be one without the other or nothing is what comes from this story.

Q - Is abortion moral or immoral? Is it against Cosmic rule or not?

A - The soul is not aborted in such procedures so the act becomes non - essential. Too much emphasis is placed on the body most of the time. A shell is what most are, eliminating not the essence of the man. The soul's entrance is the deciding factor in this case.

Q - Test-tube babies. Is it right to conceive in a tube?

A - Again, it doesn't matter. The egg is then implanted in a woman and most of the time the soul doesn't enter until much later. The soul remains important, not how or where the body or shell was received.

Q - What is Justice?

A - Earthly or Heavenly?   Earth Justice is a concept with no foundation in Truth; therefore,   no   good   comes   from   this source.   Your earth considers justice to be one of an eye for an eye - punish those who have lost their way.   Not good. They should be helped to find their path, these poor soldiers of negative outcomes. Earth   justice   remains   actually   an <u>injustice</u> to all who are involved.   Maybe the one who has done the wrong should live and help the one he has wronged. This would save time in the incarnation process.

Heavenly justice is of the Light, letting each and every one know of the Light, allowing them the Divine Right of helping others.   Heavenly justice is a way of providing true meaning for one's soul.   One's purpose for existence would be known for it is allowed through the thought form of Heavenly Justice.   All is just on this plane, have no fear of that.

Q - What is the purpose of Punishment?

A - The purpose of punishment is not of learning or making better for a negative outcome once received.   It is one of promise for the future of a society which would have none if nothing were done to these soldiers of the negative outcome. Society, at this time, cannot see to other solutions so punishment is only a   survival   tactic   for   others   not concerned with the growing or learning of the soldier himself.

Q - Why isn't there peace on earth?

A - Oh, my small children, peace will never come until all souls are united and one with the Light. Ignorance of the Light causes nonpeace, individuality, and community.

Q - Why do we live in a violent culture?

A - A violent culture? Well, many reasons, as so many of darkness reside on that plane. It saddens us here to see this situation. Hatred serves no purpose and that is why evil came from such a source. Repayment in a next life must be made, but until all realize this, a vicious circle it remains. Some of the point to our work is to help change this type of living.

Q - What is the purpose of war?

A - Triumph. For these men who sit at heads of countries do not do the fighting themselves. They send men of blind following who need not "be" in the bigger scheme of things. But as long as people put others in office and allow them to control actions as they do, there will be war. Maybe if toy soldiers would become "real" men, then there would be no need for war.

We understand the need for protection from men of darkness but this seems not to be the case in most instances.

Q - Is nuclear war a real possibility?

A - Nuclear devastation will always remain part of the accurate truth as long as there exist men of darkness. No real threat from higher powers, only men of the shadow side of the Light.

Q - Should we try to begin and maintain relationships with others in the Soviet Union for the purpose of global peace?

A - I feel that this a fine way to go, yet my question is, could we not start with peace on a smaller scale? For individual peace would bring worldwide peace. And so many individuals on earth are so "un" at peace that it seems to be a great jump without a middle ground before this can be accomplished. We may take individual healing and, in that, it will bring a peace of its own.

Q - What purpose does Russia and America serve?

A - It serves for different life experiences in soul. For soul knowledge must be obtained in this way. The two varied lifestyles are of the polarity nature. Maybe one will come back American, the next time Russian, the next time American, to see - until each and every soul has experienced each. Then the compassion, the understanding, and the peace that all wish for may occur.

Q - Are homosexuals more developed or less developed than heterosexuals? And what about transsexuals?

A - Homosexuals are of a special quality. They are ones who cannot put their androgynous aspect aside when they incarnate. They know of the One so intimately, even on a lower level, that they cannot separate their sex.

Usually when one is born, one knows what sex one is because one previously picked it for one's own need and lesson knowledge. Very rapidly most learn to forget their archetypal selves and pick and stay with the sex they decided on before life.

Homosexuals retain knowledge of the spirit plane - not enough to know what they are doing - but enough to confuse themselves considerably throughout their earth life.

Transsexuals made a decision before life and it seemed not to be the "right" one. So they changed to accommodate their need or want. Sometimes it is a person's first incarnation to one sex or the other and they find it too uncomfortable, not familiar enough, so they take on the sex that is more familiar, known, and comfortable. Needless to say they must eventually come back as the sex they cannot find comfort in.

Q - Are people affected by the Stars?

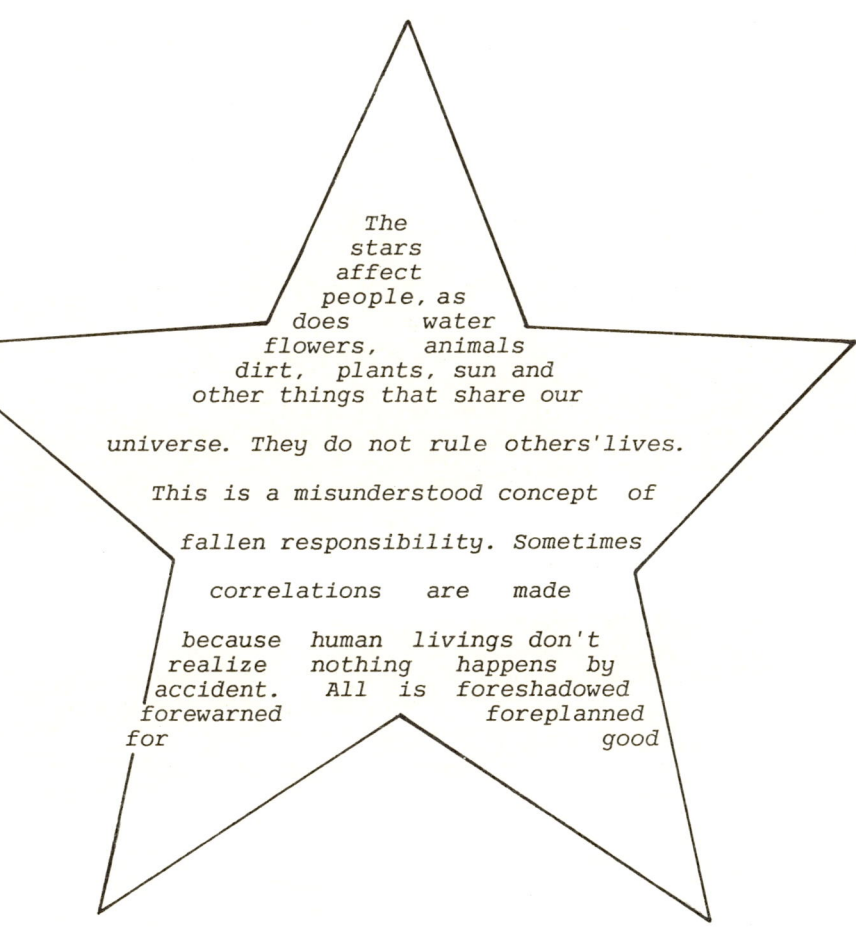

The
stars
affect
people, as
does   water
flowers,   animals
dirt, plants, sun and
other things that share our

universe. They do not rule others' lives.

This is a misunderstood concept of

fallen responsibility. Sometimes

correlations   are   made

because   human   livings don't
realize   nothing   happens by
accident.   All   is   foreshadowed
forewarned   foreplanned
for   good

Q - Why are there two different sexes on earth?

A - One or the other must be used to bear children. Woman was chosen and given more pain power, endurance and nurturant ability. There is a difference between men and women on earth. Each is a part of the whole. This you can understand. Each soul gets a chance to experience one or the other in order to be whole. This is good.

Q - What is the purpose of marriage?

A - The purpose of marriage is one of unattached giving, of loving another more than yourself. Same principle as mother and child. But poor father, he only has wife in this way.

Q - Monogamy - is it cosmically moral?

A - It is only a concept and a practice in the human body. It does not have a cosmic reality. For then it is not right or wrong, good or bad. It is a choice, it is a growing process.

If you can remember that growth is our main purpose in all areas whether it be spirit, soul, mind, body, then you will have your answer. If you feel a growing, if you feel an understanding, if you feel a comfort with the way your life is going, then this remains a right choice. If it is not a right choice, you will know it.

Q - What is the greater purpose of divorce?

A - Divorce is that of self-punishment. For in punishing another, we punish ourself, of course.

Q - Why do men batter women?

A - This is not a general answer. There are many reasons for such a situation to occur.

1 - The man has been hurt somehow by that woman. She decides before coming back that this is the way she will repay such an act.

2 - They both have hurt and despised each other in other lives and a mutual agreement made long ago will be forefilled.

3 - The man is a soul gone wrong and has not come to his senses. The woman is caught and cannot see her way out past this lost soul. This is the saddest of circumstances for all concerned. A cycle that someday will need to be broken.

Q - Why does prejudice still exist?

A - Prejudice exists because not all people have repaid debts of lessons needed and not learned. Once all is repaid, repaired, made new, no need for such harsh lessons will exist.

Q - What is the greater purpose, or the Cosmic lesson of such massive horrible suffering as the famine in Ethiopia?

A - We are glad that earth point questions, "problems" have been raised. Ethiopia, as any famine country, has a very special purpose on earth. These individuals come for quite an evolved lesson for they have been in time of plenty many lives. This purpose that they have decided to forefill on earth is one of waiting and watching and seeing if the underevolved souls who have come down are willing to help, have found a way to help, are caring enough to help, those they think they do not know. The closer the rest of the world gets to caring for individuals on a greater level, the closer they feel to being connected with these individuals in these famine places, the less there will be need for these highly evolved spirits to come down with souls into bodies that require poverty situations.

Q - What is the purpose on earth for desert areas Janith?

A - To show the people of earth exactly where they have gotten to in their understanding of barrenness.

Q - Will the land masses change in our lifetime?

A - They are changing now.

Q - Do you have anything you'd like to say about the problem of pollution on earth?

A - Concentration must first be on internal pollution of the individual organism. This is where to begin.

Q - And how to begin?

A - How to begin? By knowing oneself, knowing one's intention, raising one's consciousness, becoming of clear mind, soul, emotion, and physicality.

Q - Has food much to do with it?

A - Can we intake without polluting? Of course.

Q - Do microwave ovens have a negative effect on us?

A - Quite a good question! For technology is not always of the highest good. I may say that these microwaves make upside down the order of things as far as when we speak of positive, negative ions, moving around, radiating. They play with the natural order of things.

Q - The Challenger space shuttle explosion, can you tell us in the highest sense why this occurred?

A - I may say that it was quite a humbling experience for all concerned on earth plane. For it was a signal as well as for the highest good of all involved. It was obviously time for the crew to transcend, and they had decided to make a quite good lesson for earth plane. Yet, I do not think earth plane got this so well. But the objective is to let ones know that <u>inner</u> journeys will provide outer happiness, outer fulfillment, ultimate goal, rather than outer, upper journeys.

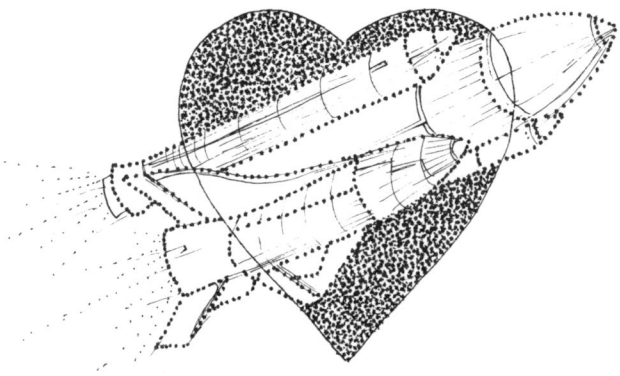

Q - Could you answer what Extra Terrestials are and tell us why they seem to be trying to make contact with us now?

A - Extra? I may say that they are not extra. They are brother friends, they are learning and growing. And communication at this time is very important to recognize. Not only the existence of spirit and other realms, but of other planetary beings. There is only good intent.

Q - Are there other galaxies?

A - Yes, there are nine, not including the spirit galaxy.

Q - Is there life on other planets?

A - Oh yes. Different life. Past, present, and future life and no life as you know it.

Q - Are there animals on other planets Janith?

A - Of course. Yet, different. Bungles. Quite cute are these little furry creatures of a ball-like nature.

Q -Bungles instead of pets? Are there others?

A - Bungles and other pets. Shumeys, with pastel hair. Little shumeys, very kind and loving. Whenever one raises consciousness off the earth plane, there are quite nice surprises.

Q - Can air travel affect human beings magnetic fields?

A - I may say that it jumbles some, yet it does not take away or give to, so it is of little consequence, except of a disorientation nature. I think this is called "jet lag."

Q - What is a parent's true responsibility to their children?

A - To keep them out of earthly harm and to help them in whatever they are doing. Parents may help children discover their true soul's purpose. This is a good way to go with such responsibility.

It is not a parent's job to steer a child in their direction for this steers one away from his own true purpose and need for lesson knowledge.

Q - How should parents deal with difficult adolescents?

A - Parents? We will call them "Helper Guides of the Third Dimension." Their task is this. They may guide and protect, aid and love - but they may not take over responsibility for another's life choices.

Once information is given of the good, the Light, and the right way of life (love), then one must sit back as one does at the cinema and watch, enjoying lessons being learned by his/her little one.

Remember, pain is growth and growth is the lesson which will expand and aid in our everlasting Light (life). So, parents (Helper Guides of the Third Dimension) do not despair if the movie has an unhappy beginning, middle or end, for this is consistent with growth and that is the main objective. Not happiness. For happiness, peace and contentment only comes from higher growth. One must begin and fall and run in order to get to the highest rung on the ladder.

Q - Why are smoking, drinking, and drugs detrimental?

A - Smoking allows holes in body for energy not once permitted into the aura, into the chakras, into the esseric bodies. Smoke is a repellent for all, not only for wrong ones, so it makes communication harder to take place for we must fight through a cloud of smoke for the essence to speak to.

Drinking alters consciousness to the extent that only the negative appears. Can be carried into the soul at times of drinking. Takes time for this to go far.

Drugs have an androgynous manner about them. Some inhibit communication; some aid communication.

Q - How can drugs help to break a soul/spirit connection?

A - There are many forms of alternate consciousnesses in your world. There are certain types of these chemicals that remain harmful to the connection between soul and spirit for they are a physically altering drug, not a mind altering drug. Certain physiological changes happen when something is taken such as tranquilizers, cocaine, or "angel dust,"as they would like to say. These are not mind-expanding drugs. They are more physical, more rational, in their base. So they then connect solely with mind and body which brings you a little farther from soul/spirit connection. If that connection is not very strong to begin with, this type of action just might be the straw that broke the camel's back, as it were.

Q - Janith, what happens to addictions at Death?

A - Addictions' at death? Well if ones are still attached, they must be spoken to, spoken of with the counselors we have here. Almost like a "releasing addictions board." Most give it up on the way out of body. They leave it with body. You may consciously do this at death.

Q - Just by intention?

A - Of course. Just...?

Q - Does the release board ever function with people on earth?

A - I do not see of a purpose for this.

Q - So that you can release things that you don't want to keep with you?

A - That you do not <u>need</u> to keep with you. You do not wish to release until they are done. And they are only done when you see fit to release.

Q - Can you tell me the purpose obesity
serves in the "knowing" of a soul? Or
the cosmic lesson?

A - There is not such a thing as cosmic
lesson in this way for it has purpose yet
purpose is interpreted from a societal
point of view. Yet, I must say, each
individual is learning something
different and needed that incorporation
to be able to learn his/her purpose in
that lifetime.

Q - Is it the same with Bulimia and
Anorexia?

A - These two eating disorders that you
speak of are more in the way of cosmic
purpose. Bulimia is one of taking in too
much; in any way, form or shape, yet it
takes form of food for that is tangible
to understand at the time. It is more
taking than giving and not knowing how to
resolve that in relationships so it is
learned through self.

Q - And Anorexia is just the opposite
then?

A - Anorexia is quite a different
disorder for it is a person's non -
acceptance of soul purpose in this
lifetime. For they are hoping to waste
away, if you will, the life they have
been given, this life.

Q - What is nature?

A - Nature is two things: flowers, trees, bees and other livings than human. But also we speak of the nature of man. The nature of man is to be one with the Light. The nature of man is to engulf all that is. The nature of man is good, not evil. Only when one ignores his true nature does it turn to dust.

Q - Why do whales beach themselves and die?

A - For they are creatures of a non violent nature and when it is time in their soul's purpose for returning to the One, they do so.

Q - Is it right to shoot horses?

A - I may say that shooting horses is a judgement. Is it right? It is done to help ones out of their misery. They are not learning from such a situation so all is fine.

Q - Should animals be used for scientific experiments?

A - Animals used for scientific experiments are sad. People must learn by trial and error that it is never a good thing to hurt other livings. But your planet does many harmful things to livings.

Q - What is Science?

A - Science - a changing, growing reality made up by man to explain his present surroundings according to his limited three-dimensional knowledge. Science enables the unspiritual man to live comfortably in his own illusion world. It is only bad if and when it stunts growth.

When <u>limited</u> to a science way of thought, one cannot see and search for other answers to different, or the same, questions. Science is a make-believe knowledge of explanation. Once a person thinks only in this way, surely he will not come to see the Light in this lifetime of his.

Q - Why are we a left-brain (rational, logical) society?

A - We? You, not I, are of a left-brain society. Not because of some undying need to make sense of the world around you, but to claim sense and power of your own. If you were to seek sense, it would be a different story; therefore, a different end. Sense is all around, only our meanings vary from place to place.

Q - How can one boost right-brain (creative) thinking?

A - Shots to the right brain will come through creativity in a higher sense of the word's meaning.

Q - **What is Time?**

A - *Time is the greatest of the illusion concepts. Time is a useful tool for human structure. Time is also useful in helping evil entities play their games of darkness, where human livings are the play pieces in the game. Time aids in the left of brain (sequential, rational) to function on the earth plane. Time is a structure of a world which would have none without. Time will no longer be needed when all experience the Light. All will feel good with this. Time - a straightjacket for the unevolved.*

Q - **Why are there Satan worshipers?**

A - *Satan worshipers are of the worst kind of evil for they idolize a concept which is against all good. Please let these ones know that there is no such entity as Satan. He is only a model, a false combination of all that is self and commonly destructive.*
  1 - Knowledge of his non - existence should help in a small way. Yet, some will remain with this odyssey way of life.
  2 - Society will realize only through action and words that good is more powerful and beneficial for all in the life state.
  Movies, books, any form of media may portray healthy forms of positive action. But this must be done in a strong way for now good is associated with meek and bad (evil) with powerful. Change this concept and herein lies our key to success in evil areas.

Q - **Why is there so much sexual abuse now which causes so much suffering in this country?**

A - *Again, this is a sad way of learning. It is unfortunate that so many of our souls feel the need to somewhat disconnect from what is higher spirit teaching them. Once that soul has taken off on a trip of its own it becomes very caught up in physical and has no spiritual nature to guide its action. So, it runs rampant through society hurting the very innocent, the very naive and the very connected to spirit. Hurting this remains as it should, for this connection must be maintained as stronger. In trying to reach these poor soldiers of the negative outcomes you must must make that connection stronger. Once that connection is stronger, the knowledge will automatically integrate into that soul and things will stop where they should.*

Q - **Then maybe I must ask you Janith, what is the cosmic reason for sex?**

A - *Don't you see that a man abusing a child is his basic want to connect to that self, that feeling of wholeness, of non-separateness. A child is the representation of the Whole, of the All, of back to where it was good.*

Sex remains that, no matter who participates in this action. It is a reminder, it is a connection when that connection is not strong enough between the soul and the spirit. For two souls, having pieces of their own spirit connection integrating together make a bigger connection to the Whole.

Q - Does a female bring in a mothering
nature or is it culturally developed?

A - Depending on how many past lives this
"mother" has attained. So your mothering
instinct would be quite stronger as a
baby child if you have had several
children in past lives and have come back
more quickly.

Q - Is there a male counterpart in the
nature of this feeling such as "paternal"
instinct?

A - Of course. This has been quite
negated. For believe it or not, the
paternal instinct is much more
unconditional; is much less restrictive.
Men trust universe quite more than women
do. Women feel they have more power over
universe. For truly, if I can give life,
can I not give everything?

Q - How come there are so many runaway
children?

A - I would like to call them run-to
children. For they are not running away,
they are seeking to find. And they are
only, in the physical world, showing each
and every one in that plane that this is
what it is all about. They are running,
they are finding, they are seeking. The
home that they thought was there has not
been, and they are looking for it. And
they may find it in different ways. If
home is to be known as something that
occurs after this life, and the building
of a house can have a feeling of home,
then maybe less run-to children would
occur.

Q - How come there are so many homeless people? What is the purpose of that?

A - Much the same as others in poverty situations. For does not each and every person in New York have an extra room for this one to live in?

Q - Could you please tell us what the cosmic purpose of suffering is Janith?

A - Cosmic purpose? Purpose serves more of human livings' need. For a greater purpose, there is no such thing. When consciousness is raised high enough, suffering does not exist.

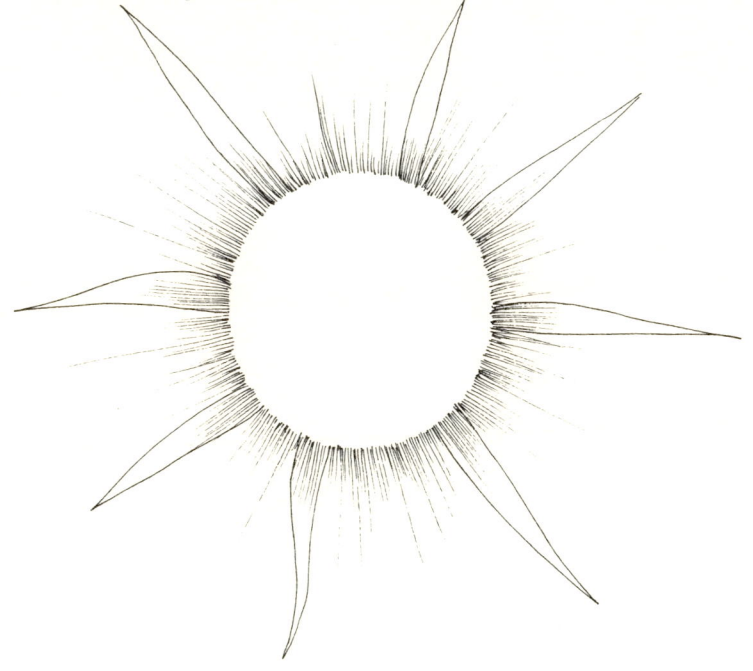

PERSONAL DISCOVERIES

*"Free will is a choice
gift from God; a gift of
freedom to learn, to choose,
to right once wronged."*

JANITH

Since the time of Freud and Jung, we've acknowledged that man is more than body. The disciplines of Psychology and psychiatry are based on the understanding that man is also mind. But man is not only mind and body. Man is also soul/spirit. And only recently have we begun to recognize the importance of this aspect of man and to include it in his healing.

How many of us, after realizing that success in the outside world doesn't necessarily bring inner happiness, spend much of our lives trying to rediscover ourselves? We do this by learning - whether through education or experience - and one day find that we've arrived back at the very place we started as children. Often, in our searching, we come upon tools which help us live our lives more happily and we develop a belief system and a way of perceiving that makes our life more meaningful. Hopefully, that is what the best psychotherapists help us to do when we encounter obstacles.

Janith's answers to the questions that usually fit into the categories of psychology and individual personal growth help in a broader way to give meaning and explanation to our experiences. These answers are included in this chapter in the hope that they will help on your journey.

Many of us who have had personal experience with Janith have come to realize that she is not only an angel, or spirit of creative communications, but also a valuable therapist and guru.

Q - Why do people have such a hard time deciding what it is in life that they are supposed to do?

A - If human livings knew their purpose for existence, the challenges and tests of sincerity would be split in half. Life is a series of trials and errors and only by listening to your true soul, your higher self, will a person find his/her reason for existence this time around. Life on earth is not supposed to be easy. Only to teach one well and for one to learn well. This is the reason for being on such a plane.

Q - Wouldn't it be better if everyone was born with the knowledge of who they are and what their reason for being here is?

A - Oh sweet children, easy/better it could not be, knowing the nature of humankind as I do. They could not accept such knowledge with the same intensity they learn it. Besides, born you are with the knowledge of the purpose for your existence. Too fast you forget and spend the rest of your lives rediscovering what is always within your reach. You know that money which is given is taken more lightly than money which is earned. This concept holds true throughout life. Understand?

Q - How can your advice be put to practical use?

A - It begins and it ends with trust. Unless there is trust, there is no such thing as practical use. And in that practical use there must be knowledge of the Light. Once there is knowledge of the Light there is an inner voice which leads the way and practicality will become apparent.

Q - Someone once said that there's a path of wisdom and a path of pain and that we can choose the way to learn. Is this so, and how can one choose the path of wisdom?

A - Learning of the Light, the continuous learning, growing within the Light and the All - Knowledge will always keep you on the path of wisdom. When this is ignored, there is still an opportunity for growth throughout life.

We talked of obstacle way. If not recognized as such, that becomes one with tragedy. When the obstacles are ignored, when one is tripping over obstacles without noticing, a tragedy must happen, therefore, teaching in the highest form.

Q - How can people be helped to live more in the "now?"

A - Help in this matter is not essential. Help in this matter does not teach the lesson of the now, does not teach the lesson of non - waiting. Does not teach, that is why it is not essential.

Q - **What is imagination?**

A - *Imagination combines soul, mind, and emotions. Depending upon which one becomes dominant within such a person, different things may be true. If you are asking if psychic ability is the same as imagination, the answer is difficult. Yes and No.*

Yes, because you are allowing your higher self to know of other things and have other sights. No, because if a human living is having earthbound fantasies, using his mind/imagination, then I doubt we have anything to do with such a situation. But nothing is absolute on your plane. There is mind imagination, emotional imagination, and soul imagination.

Q - **Are a child's imaginary friends other worldly or are they part of mind or emotional imagination?**

A - *Most of the time the child is just acknowledging spirits who are "in the air" so to speak. This is all right. Children are protected greatly by their innocence. All is good.*

Q - **What is Wishing?**

A - *Wishing is a child's innocent way of controlling his/her own fate. But it only aids good intent, not action.*

Q - What are dreams?

A - Dreams are stepping stones toward the Light, the All - Knowledge. If used correctly, they can be wonderful. Use dreams to correct situations, to amend old wrongs, to repair broken souls.

Q - Is there a name for the field where people meet in the dream state?

A - Again, you are making a distinction between a place, a time, a space. You can call it anything you wish to call it for it is not a distinct entity. It is as it is. "Field," if you want to call it a field. If you want to call it a baseball diamond, it is a baseball diamond, if you want to call it a car, it is a car. It does not matter. It is just the meeting that becomes the importance, not the place.

Q - Do people meet each other, as they know each other, if there is "each other" in this place?

A - Individual minds, individual souls connect. We know of this, you know of this. There is a familiar feeling when one has met another in dream or at another time space. But it is also All. For any thing that is met by two minds, two souls, is met by the Universal One, the All - Knowledge.

Q - What is dream flying?

A - Exactly what it is.

Q - What is a nightmare?

A - A nightmare is a human living confronting his/her own shadow side during sleep for it is still too uncomfortable to face this during what human livings see as their day reality.

Q - Do children have their own soul's purpose? How can parents discipline them without interfering with this process?

A - This is quite a good question. I may say, of course, children have soul's purpose. Where do we think they would get it from if not from spirit blueprint once they come in? I may also say that discipline comes from fear vibration. Fear of society, fear of wrong, fear of misbehavior in the way of "shoulds." Unconditional love is the only answer here for if you are not coming from fear, no matter what they do, it is fine. It is their soul's purpose. Trusting the universe is quite important in parenting these days.

Q - What age would it be appropriate to open children to the world of spirit?

A - Speaking of spirit to the very young and growing, and building this foundation of a new reality, is quite essential. I may say that this may start as early as questions asked - which may be two years.

Q - Why are grandparents so important to
the growth of children?

A - Unconditional love is mainly what
grandparents should be providing for they
do not come from a fear vibration for it
is not their job to raise these children.

Q - Janith, what is Fear?

A - A very complicated question. Fear
combines all knowledge of past, present,
and future. The soul remembers a past
life experience, an end result, then
tries to apply it in a present day
situation. This should try to be
avoided.
    Fear can be healthy to some extent,
because, in man, fear breeds respect.
Other than that, fear should be overcome.

Q - Janith, could you please give us some
straight talk about judgements?

A - There is much to say on human
judgements. For this allows one not to
look truthfully at oneself. This is
truly the only reason for judgement - to
make one feel illusion better about
oneself. For it is not truly better, it
only appears this way.
    Judgement about anything can be
released if fear is released.

Q - Why is it that so many people feel they have to move away from a house in which a tragedy has happened?

A - Because human livings have not differentiated between illusion and reality. The <u>feeling</u> is that the space provided is the unsure ground they walk on. Yet, the place they live in doesn't really contain the evils that seem to exist. Once they leave, it becomes easier for the fear is not as developed as when in that space. It is only an illusion from one home to another home. It is all really the same.

Yet, fear can allow entities of a mischevious nature to play illusion games in that particular area for the fear is elevated beyond earth level.

Q - Can you explain fear of mice to us, Janith? And a fear of snakes?

A - A fear of mice comes from that of different lives. Some have been tortured with, some have been found to have been in poverty situations where they died a rat death. It also comes from a lower consciousness. And it is the fear of that lower consciousness that signifies whether the person is really living life's soul purpose or not.

Snakes are a little different. In the first two cases they may be seen as above mentioned. Yet, in the third case, I may say that it is a fear of slipping away into <u>another</u> consciousness.

Q - Why are people so afraid of the paranormal, the spiritual, the higher self?

A - The unknown is always a problem with human livings. That is why we wish to make known this important information.

Q - Janith, please tell us the benefit of switching from a Fear vibration to a Love vibration.

A - I may say that it does not only have one benefit. It has <u>benefits</u>. For any time one switches from fear to love, the outcome will be assured.

Q - Why do people badger each other?

A - People badger each other because of a lack in understanding of another's feelings. People badger each other for a revengeful way of thinking it is. Do not fault those of this mind for their time has not come for the Light.

Q - Why do people envy each other?

A - Jealousy is a sad way to leave. It's the same thing people do with the Christ idol. Envy him in his All - Knowledge. No need for envy if one has taken responsibility for one's own growth life.

Q - What is Patience?

A - Patience is the strong belief that everything will come to you as it may. It is not patience in waiting - for there is no waiting with such a belief. Love is the theme, unattached, undivided.

Q - Janith, what is Loyalty?

A - Loyalty is a strong connection of soul to All, the One, God. Loyalty is a universal concept; loyal to God, loyal to self, loyal to all. The highest form of loyalty is non-selective in its origin.

Q - What is Kindness?

A - Kindness is a simple gesture of love, a completion of intent in which the basis lies in love. This is good. But we are speaking of devout kindness, not simplistic, superficial kindness only done for the sake of being kind. This becomes patronizing in its nature.

Q - What is the significance of people's eye color if there is one?

A - If eyes are the mirrors of the soul, color would tell you something about soul. I may say it is much easier to read soul through lighter colors.

Q - What is Pain?

A - Pain exists on many levels, the highest being of soul pain - deep centers are touched in the process of growth. Physical pain stems from illusion, the illusion of a false reality, a limited reality. Stop, look, and listen and you shall find physical pain does not have to be endured. There are many ways physical pain can be overcome.

    1 - Astral

    2 - Breaking through illusion of body shell.

    3 - Simply do not accept the pain.

There have been many experiments on pain tolerance. It's not the tolerance which differs, it's the human livings knowledge on higher levels of how not to accept pain in this way. But once pain is great enough, a person becomes weak in his listening power, to his higher knowledge, and loses the connection of that knowledge. Therefore, pain is felt.

Q - When people complain of a pain in the back of their neck, is this a blockage of communication on either a physical or spiritual level?

A - Or is someone in their life being a pain in the neck? It has to do with communication for if this is true, they must speak it and then the communication would occur. So ultimately communication is being blocked.

Q - What is Luck?

A - Luck is one's following his own soul's way. Luck is hearing the whispers of the soul. Good luck is right way. Bad luck is obstacle way.

A run of good luck means you have followed your good way for a great many miles. But suddenly there's a fork in the road and, Oops!, wrong choice. Therefore, springs turn of luck until you stop, look at life and your decisions past, and find that fork once again to take the other road. There, you are now on the right way again and a run of good luck begins once more.

Q - Is there any correlation between success and the right path?

A - Money, success, and popularity have nothing to do with right or wrong path. For a poor farmer may be following his right path much more directly than a rich, dishonest politician or businessman is following his.

Q - Can you give us some comments on money as an energy exchange?

A - I may say that money is a manifestation of an energy output, input. It is important on spiritual path for it must be seen as a balancing factor. For when you have something to give, there must be a taking, or it is not of a balancing nature. One must learn to incorporate both aspects without any judgement and feel as good of giving as of taking.

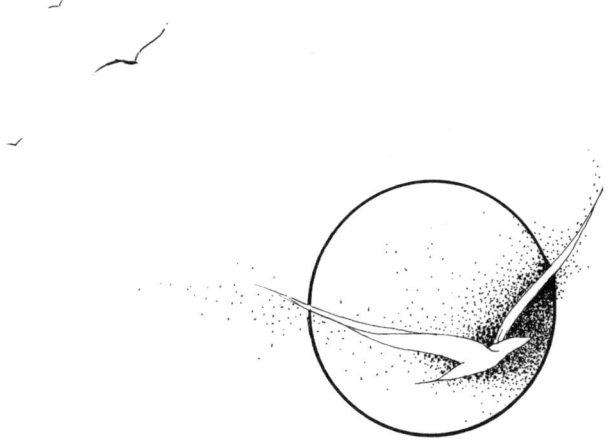

Q - What is Freedom?

A - *Flying as a dove flies is freedom. Crying as a baby cries is freedom; loving as a mother does is freedom; working as a father does is freedom; dying as a grandmother does is freedom. Trying as a brother does is freedom. Every time a lesson is learned, freedom for soul is a little closer.*

Q - What is Human Instinct?

A - Human instinct is a power greater than mind. It protects and guides, tells and forgives. Instinct is not confused by emotion; therefore, only right action comes from such a source. But very few listen to their true instincts which, on some level, is higher knowledge.

Human livings are so preoccupied with happiness that most do not concern themselves with growth. Truthful instinct is that little voice of unbiased knowledge which leads to higher growth patterns of the divine kind.

Q - Could you tell us what Curiosity is?

A - Curiosity is the key to discovery. Curiosity is the key to understandings. Curiosity remains a very important tool on earth to help individuals find the One. If man did not have a curious soul, a curious mind, he would not get into much of the trouble he finds himself in, but he would also not grow as fast as he might be capable of. Curiosity is one of the highest priorities in the pathway toward spiritual understanding.

Q - Could you please tell us the danger of Innocence?

A - There is a time where one has incorporated wisdom with innocence and this is the best of all possible outcomes. Yet, I may say, in total innocence, without wisdom, comes stagnation.

Q - What is Guilt?

A - Guilt is a slap on the hand by the unconscious mind. Guilt is a sorrowful sight of a situation of past importance. Guilt is a first step to lesson knowledge. Some may bypass this step and go on, others cannot.

Guilt is good in moderation as many other things are. But only if it is self imposed for therein lies the growth, not by others' judgemental guilt-provoking responses.

Overcome guilt by facing situations past and acknowledging your own responsibility to the situation. But do not overtax yourselves for then purpose is not right. Focus is wrong. Focus must remain on lesson knowledge, not mistakes. Yes, mistakes provide lesson knowledge but only if that knowledge is focused on, not the <u>fault</u> of the human livings. Also, do not make yourself's more powerful than you really are for all ispre-shown to each, and each one has a choice decision whether to accept his plan or not.

All is right then if guilt is only used as a self-imposed instrument of truth of circumstances, of lesson knowledge, once needed, now learned. For once you acknowledge negative responsibility or guilt, then you, my dear children, have learned and learned well. Now, release the guilt and go on with your lives. For no bigger guilt exists than stunting growth and, if focus is wrong, this is exactly what guilt will do.

Q - What is Free Will?

A - Free will is a choice gift from God. A gift of freedom to learn, to choose, to right once wronged, to love once not, to leave peaceful and serene. But it can also be used by men of darkness for negative decision-making process. It is a gift of the specialist kind.

Q - What is Hope?

A - Hope is a distant cry to the Divine for help in accepting lessons once learned. Hope is a series of plans to help aid in one's own understanding of a life's mission which must be taken seriously. This is where hope helps. Cries of hope will help in a divine way, for they insure life in a physical form will continue as long as hope is alive and well and living on earth.

Q - And Faith?

A - Faith is a deep want of another to take responsibility, for one's own higher knowledge is not accepted as real. Faith is not needed because if you are in touch with your real self, your higher self, as you are with your physical self, then you need not have faith. All you need is to look into the mirror of your soul to see of its existence. Faith can be a sad path of illusion. It's the following of something other than yourself and God's shining Light within. No faith is needed for all to experience the Light. Faith is only needed in religions of non-personal experience.

Q - Loss, in this world, is quite a difficult problem for us to deal with. Can you give us five helpful hints for beginning healing in the best way?

A - 1 - I must say to lose something you must have it. Stop being possessive.

2 - Loss must be redefined as Change. Not loss, change.

3 - Find the gift. There surely will be one or there would be no heavenly justice.

4 - Look to your soul and grow through the pain. This is quite helpful.

5 - Do not allow one to be seen as victim. You have made this manifestation. Now learn from it.

Q - Live plants: Janith, why are they so important to have in one's own life circle?

A - They are quite good protectors.

Q - What is Anger?

A - A very useful tool on earth. When one is angry, one sees their own inadequacies and can provide some sort of help in those areas. But I am speaking of useful anger, not blind anger. Blind anger hurts everyone and serves no purpose; therefore, evil comes from such a source.

Q - Can one direct the power of the energy of anger or worry into a positive direction so that positive things can materialize in one's life?

A - Again, the positive thought process is one that does not include anger, that does not include worry, that does not include these types of things. Anger is anger. Anger cannot be transformed. Until one gets to the place in one's growth process of being without anger, being naturally without worry, then all will materialize as a positive life for that person. Yet, still when one is on that plane of consciousness, one cannot get past that to transform, if you will, into positive energy from anger.

Q - What are emotions? And are they housed in soul memory, mind, or both?

A - They're housed within a physical organ. They're housed within mind and they are also housed within soul, plus a soul/spirit has also emotion.

Q - What is the difference between Happiness and Joy?

A - *Not too much difference except that joy has more of a spiritual nature. Happiness is more of a physical nature. That is it. It is a joy to see a small child at play or at sleep. It is a joy to watch sunsets of orange fall beneath the crashing waves. It is happiness that you feel at Christmas when you have just received that new baseball bat Dad promised you last year. It is happiness when all family members come together for a joyous occasion.*

Q - What part in life do animals play?

A - *Animals play a divine part in healing. They are genuine and real in their unattached giving. Very good friends can these ones be for those of the lonlier kind of life. Such animals are good and sweet and provide a sense of soul for those not in touch with their own.*

Q – What is the purpose of language?

A – There is a language that is not spoken that has a .very different purpose than does the spoken word. The spoken word is a very powerful tool on your plane, on your reality, for it puts out vibrations into a world that is in desperate need of positive vibrations. The spoken word is of vital importance for it can help steer the human race toward a better beginning.

The other language is that of the soul and some of this is recognized on your plane as art, as music, as touch. We also have a language, if you would like to call it, in our reality which is <u>known.</u> It does not make a sound, it does not carry a specific meaning, yet, it is necessary for our understanding of each part of the One.

Q – What do you call the language of spirits?

A – The language of spirits is one of transformation.

Q - What are archetypes? Where do they come from, and how can you tell the difference between soul purpose and getting caught in an archetype?

A - Archetypal ideas, presence, mind, are basically what the human living likes to see as a need not yet fulfilled, a dance not yet danced, a performance not yet performed. It is only an aspect of a deeper sense of soul acknowledgement and this is good.

Q - Could you please explain from your knowledge, what is the thing that we call "ego?"

A - I think much of the time human livings confuse ego with the greatest "I" and that is not to be the case. Ego remains a configuration of mind, rational mind, of past experience that is interpreted through rational mind as a "now" experience. It is a person's interpretation, from rational mind, about soul and its purpose.

Q - Then why does crisis or tragedy seem to dissolve or destroy that ego?

A - It doesn't. It only destroys that person's perception. It only destroys what that mind thought that soul was about. Once mind is disrupted in its rational thinking, as it were, the soul is seen as exactly what it is and what it's there for.

Q - What is Mind?

A - Mind is a clinical state of being. Mind is a factual machine of data input. Do you mind the mind? Mind can be confused so easily without thought voice of soul to help it. Mind has nothing to do with information without emotion or spirit to help guide it with a strong hand. Did you know that one may speak through soul, one may think through soul, one may make decisions through soul? That is why people in coma should never be taken off life support.

Q - How do you differentiate between brain and mind, Janith?

A - I speak of brain when I speak of physical. I speak of mind when I speak of consciousness.

Q - Janith, may I have a definition of consciousness?

A - It is a way of being. It is a way of considering yourself to be. It is a way of communication with soul mind through thought process of a similar kind.

Q - What happens to rational mind in shock, Janith?

A - *Blank. It goes blank. It has a shut down mechanism which has not been recognized in your medical community yet. This shut down mechanism allows for that soul to speak clearly of its intent, of its purpose, of its goal and therefore allows spirit/soul connection to become louder so that mind can listen without speaking, as it were. For when mind is speaking it is so much harder for soul/spirit connection to be heard.*

Q - Could you please explain what intuition is?

A - *Intuition is a communication of soul to spirit. It is a hearing of that communication being applied to a present day situation. Yet if it comes through mind, which most of the time it does not surpass, then it can be misinterpreted. If it can come directly from that spirit/soul connection, it is truthful and must be listened to.*

Q - How much should we trust in rational mind and how much in intuitive resistance?

A - *I feel that intuitive resistance is only underdeveloped warning. I may say that if something rubs one the wrong way then stay away from such a source. For if it is a needed practice, if it is a needed thing to happen on physical, in, spirit, or on soul level, it will come back in a different way that may be more of your liking.*

Q - How does one know when to trust intuition as truth, or whether it's in some way confused with ego?

A - You must know yourselves well enough to know if you are still confusing and processing through mind on the way to the knowledge. If you feel you are well enough with soul and hearing enough to experience that as a truth, then it will not be confused with ego mind.

Q - How can a therapist help or harm with the discounting or validation of a patient's paranormal experiences?

A - Labels are used in many ways upon the earth that can be of harm. Yet, I may say that truly depending on what one is ready for, is the therapist one will go to.

To give an example: If one has had a "paranormal" (funny idea) experience and one seeks and finds a therapist who calls it "schizophrenia", this is definitely not accidental. This one is having a test of internal truth vs. external truth.

But, if one goes to a therapist who can understand, then one is just looking for the validation one will find.

Q - Could you please explain the difference between psychotherapy and spiritual counseling?

A - Spiritual counseling is a much more evolved way of dealing with unlimited problems in an unlimited way. For if human livings had limited problems, psychotherapy would be just fine.

Q - Can you tell us why groups such as AA are so helpful and healing on the earth plane while others are not?

A - I may say that AA is quite a good example of the beginnings of wholeness, of looking at the individual as three parts, not only two. It includes spiritual, and spiritual is the only place that can finally pull one out.

Q - Why is flower arranging, sculpting, and painting therapeutic and does it aid in the reconnection to spirit?

A - It aids in the reconnection to spirit only if that spirit is of a Creative nature. For if it is of another nature, painting, sculpting, or flower arranging, only becomes an act of nurturance, of nurturing creative flow. This is good, yet it is not a reconnection.

Q - Can you make some comments on the feminine mother goddess energy and the masculine sun god and moon god aspects as they apply to psychology and other healing therapies?

A - I may say that we are speaking of balance. We are speaking of the integration of feminine and masculine principals as psychology calls them. I may also say that they are within every one, every "I." To be balanced in any life one must have mother goddess energy and moon god energy for it totally becomes the God energy when in balance.

Q - Janith, is there such a thing as true love and what shape does it take on earth?

A - I do not feel on earth, at this time, it comes in the form of Prince riding on horse anymore. I may say that it comes in small children, in handicapped people, unconditional loving people, and sharing. It does not come in concrete form of a man friend.

Q - Does that mean all the Princes are gone, Janith?

A - There is a Prince and Princess in each of you. Find that, and love that aspect, and you will have what you wish.

*Q - Janith, there are children who don't
have any concept of self - as "I, yet,
they can see "you." What is this
situation and how can it best be helped?*

*A - Ah! I may say that Janith is going to
have to be quite precise, I can see, with
this makeup-setup.*
   *First, I must say, this is two
spirits, coming down in unification, yet,
it also has two physical bodies. The
spirit in unification is of one parent or
the other. Does not have to be mother,
quite important. This is U. At certain
point in child life there had been
agreement to separate into two separate
"I's." Neither soul is taking
responsibility for that.*

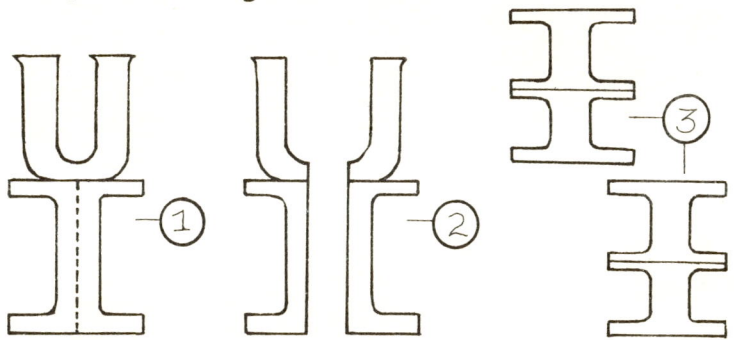

Q - How can this best be helped?

*A - By the parents listening to child.
For child will tell all.*

*Q - Is there a label that we use for
these children?*

*A - I may say label is too illusive.
It will not cover all these unifications.
So you must listen to child's word of I
or you. If you hear "you" much too often,
time to start building "I."*

Q - How can one begin to rebuild the greater I? The lesser I?

A - I may say that the greatest I has to be built from the ground up. So, for the lesser I, we must start with physical being in joyous exercise - to have soul feel physically joyous, to then have that connection bonded so strongly that it can bring us up to where soul does begin to meet spirit. Then meditation is quite a good tool.

Q - Can you tell us what is meant by "the child within?"

A - Are we asking what Janith feels is the child within man's soul?
      The child within man's soul is that which is untouched by rational mind. That which is pure as well as gentle and kind. It is the connection to spirit.
      The child within is our place of Truth.

Q - Can you please tell us what is meant by self-nurturance or nurturing the child within?

A - Well, if we nurture Truth, we are casting away false realities and acknowledging the one true reality which is All, The One, The Light.

Q - How does self-nurturance differ from, or connect with, selfishness?

A - We are speaking of different levels of consciousness. For if we turn our selfishness into nurturing the child, then that selfishness is quite useful. If we are speaking of the superficial nature of selfishness, this becomes a karmic debt.

Q - What is selfishness, Janith? Is it taking more than giving?

A - It is taking and not giving. It is taking for sole purpose of taking. For some do take. Yet their soul purpose is to give what was once taken. If we do not take, we cannot give. I may say that selfishness is taking in and containing without letting out.

Q - What is the cause of separation anxiety?

A - Feeling unconnected to the ONE. It is quite silly for we are never separated. How can one be separated when one is part of the ONE and the ONE is part of ALL?

Q - When is one ready to leave a nest of safety and return to a growing, changing way of life?

A - When one has given away old habits, gotten rid of old thinking patterns, old programs, any new way of thinking or perspective can come into being and then this happens automatically.

Q - Janith, what is the most essential truth?

A - You. The "I" in everyone. The you in everyone. Each has his own truth that must be recognized as just that.

Q - And what is the most important thing that you have to teach us?

A - That would mean that I would dictate my truth to you. That would mean that I must interpret what you find to be most essential in your lifetime of my words. That would not be a service to you, it would be a disservice. And I am not capable of such an accomplishment.

Q - Can you please give us a definition of a basic truth?

A - A basic Truth is one that breaks all barriers to all that is Universal Mind, Consciousness, Love, Light, God.

Q - Janith, are there certain basic truths? Can you tell us what they are?

A - Of course.   There are Twelve.

  1 - God
  2 - Breath
  3 - Love
  4 - Change
  5 - Air
  6 - Water
  7 - Light
  8 - Sun
  9 - Flame
 10 - Growth
 11 - Trust
 12 - Acceptance

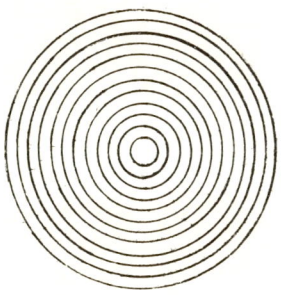

Q - What happened to earth and ether?

A - These are not basic truths, these are earth truths.   Basic truths must be able to apply to all realms, all planes, all planets.   How can earth apply to Mars? It is not a basic truth of Mars, I may say.

Q - Janith, what is Life?

A - Life is a breath from God. A breath of air, energy, and water. The breath of God is the only thing which can give life. Life is but a short moment in time. Life is a hard concept but it seems to be one with the illusion concepts also. For we are "alive"; we have life (breath of God), but we do not have physical life as you know it.

Q - What is illusion?

A - A sense of game, a false knowledge, a need to know, a false distinction between realities, a sad vision. Illusion takes many forms and guises of unknown distinction. One could be hurt tremendously playing with illusion before one is ready. This could lead to loss of mind. For when we still need that distinction, we are stripped too suddenly of all understanding. Too much too soon should be avoided (the ploy) until one is comfortable, on a soul level, of different realities being as one, the same.

Masters of Darkness use illusion as a powerful tool against humankind and as an easy outlet for a possession. Don't let this word frighten you. It is a word which means nothing to someone of good and protection.

Q - Can you list the Illusion Concepts?

A - The Illusion concepts:

> 1 - Death
> 2 - Birth
> 3 - Time
> 4 - Life
> 5 - Illusions
> 6 - Three-dimensional thinking
> 7 - Gender
> 8 - Separateness

Breaking through illusion must be done slowly, of this we warn wisely, to all who wish to complete such a task satisfactorily. Birth and death are illusions of their separateness in a time where three-dimensional thinking is used to explain them. A boy dies and a girl is born. All the same in the bigger sense of the word Life.

Q - Janith, when one understands that everything is illusion, how do you function on the physical plane?

A - One must function on earth when one realizes illusion points through this way: Wake up each morning and say:

"I am open to all possibilities for my learning and highest good. For what will take place in this day, I am not sure. But reason can be my own worst enemy, my disconnection of my Light. So, I will go today and leave myself, my true self, open to hear and find all the answers which are appropriate to this day's plans."

GIFTS DISGUISED AS TRAGEDIES

"Are you not aware that
all death is suicide?"

JANITH

Most of us have gotten so used to thinking of life as a series of problems and tragedies which bring us suffering that we spend much of our life trying to avoid the sources of that suffering. So when Janith suggested that in each of these tragedies or sufferings there was a gift, Teri and I wondered how others would accept her premise. Actually, we thought we'd just be stoned to death. But in trying to understand life from Janith's unlimited perspective, we found wisdom that we felt could help people deal in practical ways with the guilt and responsibility we all seem to take on whenever a "tragedy" occurs. Her way is very similar to the Neuro-Linguistic Programming concept of "reframing": the idea that looking at something in a different context often helps change the meaning it has for us and allows us to respond to it in a different way.

Q - Janith, what is Tragedy?

A - It is a word. That is all it is. Tragedy. A tragedy occurs on earth because human livings cannot see it is a gift. Let's redefine tragedy to be a gift from God, a gift for faster evolution. We need to change the perspective on tragedy. For how hard it is, how sad, how punished, do human livings feel with this word? Judgement is not what life and God and The One and the All Knowledge is all about. It is about gifts, it is about being able and having the opportunity to become one with the Thirteenth Master once again. This is the ultimate in blessings.

Q - When a baby or small child dies what purpose could this have?

A - Humans need purposes (reasons). Here the reasons may be:

1 - The soul has changed its mind. We are allowed some time to do this. I believe it's up to three years your time.
2 - Possessiveness: parents must learn to trust in God and let Him do as he does and still have faith.
3 - Visitations: this is when a soul returns of no karmic debt of its own, but rather to help guide those whom he's loved greatly in past lives. Most likely this child of the last example will return in some way...a new child, a lover, etc.

Q - **Why are there so many teenage suicides lately?**

A - Many souls have come back to incarnation only for a short period of time. This is the cause. For in this suicide they are knowing it is time to return. Do you not understand that all death is suicide?

Q - **What is it like the three days before you die? Is one on this plane or that plane or both? Is it a happy time?**

A - Some men are making the adjustment to death in that three-day period. Gradually more and more time is spent in another reality. The old man is quite easy to reach once senility sets in. He remembers when he was a child and talks again to us who are here to help. Quite a nice idea, I should say.

Therefore, another question has been answered. Senility, in part, is to help one's mind become closer to the Light with less resistance at the time of death.

Q - **Why, in some cases, does the spouse die soon after his/her partner?**

A - If there is a strong connection between souls of two loved ones, then this would seem a natural progression. Nothing wrong with wanting to return home (die) when a brother or sister spirit dies unless plans once made have not been fulfilled.

Q - Why is it that Loss and Death is so painful to us?

A - There is quite a lower consciousness working among the people of the earth at this time. Look at your political structure, look at your world structure. We, on this plane, see a very competitive society and competition based on who wins, who loses. That is the basis of the society, the world you live in. Yet, until human livings can see that there is no loss, that there is no death, fear will be very dominant for one should be afraid of death, one should be afraid of loss - as it is interpreted.

Yet, these things do not exist in our universe and until that is seen, I feel that all will be afraid of those things.

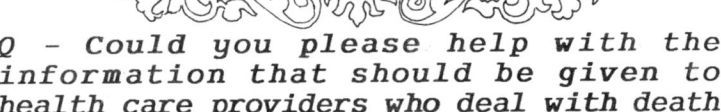

Q - Could you please help with the information that should be given to health care providers who deal with death and dying. What should be stressed?

A - Death as a transition should be stressed. Death is not an end and to look at it as an end is harmful. People are not ready not to see it as a tragedy, and yet they must understand that in their dealing with their own feelings, they will approach others in a much different light. They must understand that fear of the unknown, in any case, is most common, and must be dealt with before effective counseling for families can be done.

Q - Janith, what are the causes of disease and how can it be counteracted by us on earth at this time?

A - I may say that disease (dis - ease) either comes from mind imbalance, emotional imbalance, or past life imbalance, meaning: karma to be worked out, karma carried in, karma to be released. Diseases take many forms. I suppose at this time on earth, cancer is a big problem, yes?

Cancer shows many things that human livings negate without physical recognition of: such as deterioration of soul lesson, soul personality, betrayal of one's own soul purpose. All of these things must materialize in a way that human livings can see (form). That is why it is quite helpful to see the subtle energies for then they do not have to materialize in the physical.

Disease of mind? Dis - ease with mind is quite self-explanatory. For if we are feeling complicated, if we are feeling uncomfortable, if we are feeling disoriented when mind, emotion and soul disagree, we have a war zone, do we not? And in this area you will see physical manifestations of brain because subtle energy of mind still cannot be seen by human livings.

Emotional imbalance may appear as physical imbalance or may be seen as heart attack and heart disease. For heart is truly symbolic of emotional center.

Q - What is Cancer, the disease?

A - Cancer is the world's gift to human livings. Not a well accepted gift, but it remains a gift. A gift of unifying, a gift of despair; remember our words of growth pain.

Cancer remains a choice to learn from. Each one must learn its different message. Not only the cancer gift receiver but the ones close to such a person.

Once human livings realize that individual disease is not an enemy then we may begin to understand its use and find a different use for the same end to be received. We may be rid of cancer on your plane when those souls evolve from it and it is no longer needed.

Q - What is the lesson or purpose of brain damage?

A - The lesson is an individual one of which the gift receiver can perceive. Yet, I may say, in general, brain damage makes one come from heart.

Q - Janith, could you explain the bigger purpose of Aids and how we could help these people most?

A - Well, it is, of course, an immune system failure. And I may say that these ones have lived their lives in a very giving way, yet they have been unprotected from some of the negative, some of the external pressures. They are truly givers and of a specialist kind.
A bigger purpose? Well, of course it is a gift of God for a learning experience of growth. For it does truly break through defenses to get to the essence matter of the issues.
Help? You may just be open to the growing possibilities. And give back for they are lacking in their taking process.

Q - Can you tell us anything about allergies?

A - Allergies may be broken down into three of what you call categories. One being that of emotional disorders, emotional disruption, emotional confusion, emotional upset, not resolved, not let go. Unreleased. So it comes out in a physical way eg: sneezing, coughing. It's obviously a trying to get rid of.
The second of these would be of past life. For soul is remembering too much and not processing it in the here and now.
Three would be completely on a physical level. So get rid of what it is that makes you sneeze.

Q - What is Epilepsy?

A - Epilepsy is a disorder of sorts, also a connection the same as dreaming, with the spirit plane. Short visits with us must be maintained by the individual in order for their life to continue on earth. Most are such gentle beings from a different time. Yet, this connection causes more harm than good because the reaction human livings have is one of misconception. If these souls of epilepsy were left to feel free about their connective seizures, they would remember great amounts of knowledge from our world. This would be good.

Q - For Epilepsy. What are the most important points to stress in helping?

A - As in any other health "problem" as human livings see it, one must stress knowledge - for the unknown is what we're afraid of. One must stress non-judgement, for this could be any one of the people who are making that judgement. This is only another way of learning and learning fast. This is a greater human being, not a lesser human being, and they must see that to overcome this type of growth process, to go on, they are better human beings for what they do.

Q - What do people have to learn by being physically deformed, Janith?

A - Many who are physically deformed have much to show outside society, world, of beauty within. It truly tests ones own perceptions, own and others' acceptance, and unconditional love. And how fooled are we by outside appearances? These are very good high tests, these highly evolved souls have come to teach. Learning on their own? I may say they are learning as any other, yet they have a special purpose.

Q - What is the purpose of being deaf?

A - To hear with your heart.

Q - What is the purpose of being blind?

A - To see with your inside (insight) eyes.

Q - What is the purpose of paraplegia?

A - To learn to walk with one's astral body.

Q - What is the purpose of amputees?

A - To learn to be whole from within, not without.
Do you know that each person chooses these things in plans once made because of the lesson best shown by such a circumstance? And did you know that most don't learn even with such drastic measures?

Q - Why is Life unfair?

A - It is not unfair. Please remember, all is just from which comes learning. Life only seems unfair to those with negative outlook in growth life experiences.

Q - Why can't some people have children?

A - Some are told they can't have children by physical ones. Sometimes this is not true, yet try they don't. Some are born not able because of plans once made for lesson knowledge to be obtained. And still others may not because their turn has not come. All must be done in an orderly fashion.

Q - What are Mongoloid babies all about?

A - Oh, how cute and helpless are these beautiful Oriental like creatures! Love of other is their purpose point. Preservation of innocence is also involved in such a case.

Q - Can you tell us anything about Autistic children, Janith?

A - Autistic children may be helped by none around them for these children are the only ones who understand their own soul's purpose. Care givers of such people may only respond with love, warmth from the Light, and all is won.

Q - Why are we also so afraid of Insanity and loss of control?

A - Maybe human livings like this world as it is for if they did not, insanity would be the choice of a more advanced human being. For it is comforting, it is getting away from a lot of the earth's problems, from the devastation of the small mentalities. Insanity is a nice place to be, yet it has been labeled not good for it takes away from the competitive thinking, from the "reality" as you would call it. There is no sickness in insanity, there is no death in insanity, there is no pain in insanity. It is a wonderful way of being on your plane, a wonderful way of escaping, if you will, some of earth's realities that are not pleasant. It is not such a bad thing, yet people are fearful for it takes away their reality as they've defined it.

Q - Why does it sometimes look so painful, even for the people experiencing it?

A - It looks so painful because of our own interpretation, first of all. Secondly, they are afraid because of the society-imposed fears. If one could live their life in ignorant bliss, one would. Insanity is only painful when one realizes one is insane. If one does not realize that, and if others do not place that judgement, there is no such thing.

Q - Why does schizophrenia occur?

A - Schizophrenia, most of the time, occurs when a person chooses to come back in order for a large variety of people to hear different sights in life. This could be called mental illness, but no cure will be found by physical ones.

Q - Could you tell me the causes and the proper treatment for depression?

A - The proper treatment is laughter. Cause? I may say is one of many different reasons. Mostly, of not accepting life as a growing, changing, loving, process, gift.

Q - What is the purpose of Drug addiction?

A - The purpose of drug addiction is this: to understand a commitment to other. It doesn't matter other what/who. These ones learn only in this way. It is actually a pre-run life for the next so one may win in his learning next time around. Total love can only begin with a free and total commitment. Addiction ties them in, so to speak, to something so strongly they cannot escape from it as they could something outside their body. It must take place from within themselves. These persons may acknowledge and understand this commitment earlier than death. This is only when they can begin their rehabilitation or unattachment program for then all is right.

Q - Janith, can you tell us something about gambling? What lesson or purpose does it serve?

A - Is it not fun? And, of course, it is one with addiction, with negative side, shadow side, yet it is also one of learning to break through stagnation. For how good to be able to throw away one's security at the drop of a hat.

REINCARNATION, KARMA, EVOLUTION

"Plans once made have
openings, as does a screenplay....
Walk in, write in...you have
certain freedoms. That is the
freedom of choice."

                    JANITH

I don't remember when I began believing that it made no sense to think that the Good Lord would only allow us one chance and one lifetime to get it right and learn our lessons. Probably as soon as I, myself, became a parent and understood how many allowances I made for my own children. But as soon as I made that correlation, reincarnation seemed to be the logical outgrowth of my understanding.

After spending years sitting at the bedside of dying patients, I learned that few of us have a chance to tie up all the loose ends of our life in one lifetime. I wondered where those unresolved aspects of guilt, anger, and love, went. In a system where energy can't be created or destroyed, I figured they must be hanging somewhere, waiting for us to pick them up again and work them through.

That's how I began to understand
karma and began to believe in the
necessity of exploring our past lives.
   The model for .that in therapy is
exploring childhood memories to resolve
early conflicts in order to become a more
effective adult. Here, I just knew it
was necessary to explore the history of
past lives to become a more effective and
evolved soul in the present.

Q - What is reincarnation?

A - A soul's incarnation of previous
lifetimes which maintains a certain
criteria for the helping of knowledge
attainment and human forefillment.
Reincarnation is a growing, changing
process of an evolutionary nature. It is
a chance; an opportunity to become one
with God.

Q - Do we reincarnate with families?

A - When reincarnation occurs it is not
of consequence whether each comes back
with any other one known, for the point
is lessons to be learned, not who we
learn them with and where. If one's
consciousness is raised high enough, we
understand we are all a family. So the
answer is, yes, we do come back in groups
and families.

Q - Can humans ever transmigrate or
become animals?

A - Humans have been, in their
evolutionary process, as you call it
animal livings. It does not go backward
in evolution toward involution for the
highest good.

Q - How can we be sure there is a life
after death other than a belief system?

A - In a belief system that goes to the
depths of the soul, it then becomes a
concrete manifestation of a reality.
Yet, the only way to really discover a
life after death is to die.

Q - What is Talent?

A - Talent is left over material from previous incarnates. Talent is evolving from the past to NOW lessons learned and retained. Talent is untapped universal energy being tapped into. Talent is good for it precipitates growth.

Q - What are child prodigies?

A - Child prodigies exist for a number of different reasons:
  1 - old soul coming back for a quick trip.
  2 - Mediate soul coming back with a head start.
  3 - Beginning soul sent down too soon and remembers far too much of spirit plane to take on new learning patterns.

Q - What is a twin soul?

A - Matching set.

Q - What is a soul mate?

A - A crew member on the same journey.

Q - Is there a reason why there are two different sexes on earth?

A - When we are planning our life on earth in physicality, I may say that we must experience balance. This is what occurs in taking on the different forms of sex. We can not truly be of an androgynous nature in spirit if not learned in physical body, on earth schoolroom plane.

Q - If a person begins as spirit and stays as spirit, though I know on some level we all do, do some spirits choose not to incarnate?

A - Yes, there are some of us who were before, as you might understand, the first fish. In all areas of life, on all ships of life, there must be a captain. And that captain has to build that ship. Therefore, it seems unreasonable to assume that there were not others from the beginning that do not incarnate, do not ever see what it is to be the soul of man.

Q - Can one exist both on the spirit plane and on the earth plane at the same time?

A - Since time is an illusion, the answer must be yes. But for your understanding, the answer must be no. Not at the "same" time. For one may travel with spirit while in physical form and one may come to spirit plane while in physical form. But as I, Janith, am on spirit plane, I may communicate with human livings but I may not be incarnate at the "same" time.

Q - Between physical incarnations, Janith, can we act as guides for other less-advanced souls?

A - Truly we are not speaking of a linear or lateral process. Less, more? Only that there are those who have more to do. Please clarify this question.

Q '- Between our soul lives can our spirits act as guides for others?

A - Of course.

Q - How important are our past lives to our "now" existence?

A - How important are our eyes to see?

Q - What is the primary purpose of exploring past lives, Janith?

A - I feel that it has many primary reasons for there are essential background papers on each and every one, and until we may look into our past, how can we understand our future?

Q - How many past lives can we explore effectively at one time, Janith?

A - What is meant by effectively?

Q - For the highest good, for spiritual growth?

A - Would one study more than one thing at a time to know it fully?

Q - So you suggest we explore just one past life at a time before we go on to another?

A - I suggest that one looks internally and knows what one can absorb.

Q - Do we bring in with us, Janith, physical manifestations of disease? And, if so, how can we help to remedy this?

A - I may say that if past lives have not been explored and resolved, then, of course, you would be at dis - ease with them. I may also say that you may help by exploring, seeing, rediscovering, and mending.

Q - Do birthmarks have significance? Can they be carried on from a past life?

A - They all have some significance for they would not be there if they didn't. Some are carried on from different soul imprints. I may say that if something was not accomplished as it wanted to be in a past life, it could be carried within this. I may also say that at other times it may be a parental passing on of some special talent. For if child has a similar birthmark to parent, it could be seen as similar gift each has to share with the other.

Q - Is it possible while on earth to alter "plans once made" in order to change the outcome?

A - Plans once made have openings, as does a screenplay. Walk in, write in, you have certain freedoms, that is the freedom of choice, which is not filled in before birth. These plans once made have a basic outline of how the story will end. Yet, freedom of choice on earth can change an outcome, can change most anything including the complete opposite of what plans once made were.

Q - When are these plans once made, made?

A - In the time, in the space, provided for rest, for evaluation, for planning. It is after death, sometimes it is in dream state as a person is alive on earth, plans are being formed, plans are being thought of, plans are being lived out. In that space between life and death is where most decide what the next step will be in their growth process.

Q - And can you do that several lifetimes before?

A - Yes, because it is hard to explain that it is not a linear or lateral process we are talking about. So two, four, six lives before is really not before. It is the same.
It is hard to discuss universal concepts in the box that is labeled time, earth. What you consider to be process is different than what we consider to be process.

Q - Do we choose careers before life?

A - Chosen careers may be done before life but also may be discarded when one lands on the plane through birth. So chosen they are, predestined they are not. Usually if one's knowledge of lessons needed is great enough, the career will remain right or be close to that once chosen. For example: Nurse - Helper; Wife - Helper; Doctor - Helper.

Q - Janith, does a soul choose before it is born at what age it will die? And can that be changed during an incarnation?

A - It is quite complicated from your vision for it is all spelled out, but it is not in only one way spelled out. There are many avenues that have been offered and all will achieve the same end, the same goal. I may say that to put it more simply, maybe six roads were mapped out before and it is choice of which one to take.

Q - What is karma, Janith?

A - A circle of Light.

Q - How does it work?

A - Easily.

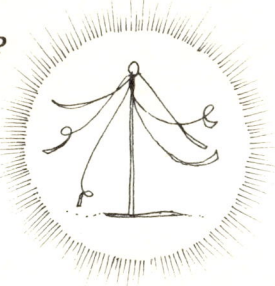

Q - Can you tell us the difference between karma and grace?

A - There isn't really a difference between too many things. The difference that I see in this question is that grace seems in human living's eyes to be <u>bestowed</u> on one, to be given to one. Karma is earned. Karma is learning. Karma is growing. Karma is giving back and taking from, and once that hits an equilibrium, then instant karma is achieved.

Q - How does writing containing evil content affect one's karma?

A - Writing with evil <u>intent</u> containing whatever content will produce negative outcomes in such a person's life. Very sad. For the ones who are capable of reporting the evil are also capable of receiving and hearing the good. There is no bigger sin than not following plans once made. From this original sin stems all other. No person's original plans contained such evil doings.

Q - Janith, what karma is being fulfilled or what lessons are to be learned by adoption?

A - Karma in this situation is individual, so this cannot be answered. Yet, I may say that the adoption of a child brings a consciousness into life on earth of family being all.

Q - What is the karmic purpose of a mother-daughter relationship? How does it differ in dynamics from a mother - son relationship?

A - Usually, the karma is one of a male female energy that has not been fully integrated into oneself. So, usually when daughter is born, she is born to help teach mother of feminine aspect. When son is born, he is helping to integrate male aspect. When there is one of each, there is quite a good balance, I must say. Also too, this is quite an individual question for there are many reasons that two souls incarnate together.

Q - Is it true that once one reaches Christ consciousness, meaning love, that all karmic debt is cancelled?

A - Is this question of reaching highest love vibrational energy? I may say you may not be working up any more "negative" karma, yet I may say you will be gaining positive.

Q - Janith, can one have too much positive karma?

A - You would not be here asking this question.

Q - Are there lifetimes in which no previous karma is being worked on, and how is this indicated?

A - On physical plane? In earth schoolroom? What purpose would there be in being separated from the beautiful Light if nothing is going to be gained and learned?

Q - In some cases wouldn't ones come down to help others?

A - Only when karma is completely finished do we have opportunities to come down to give. Quite rare.

Q - *On a Cosmic level, Janith, how is one's karma affected by suicide?*

A - *This is a funny way of looking at it, yet, it is as if instant karma has occurred. For it is the absolute physical recognition of the giving to and taking of coming together.*

Q - *Can you tell us what evolution is?*

A - *Evolution is also a circle, the outer circle of karma. I may say that it is an ongoing process.*

Q - *During evolution, over time, is the brain physiology becoming different? Are we more able to pick up telepathy or is it just an expansion of a mind set that allows us to hear the capacity that our brain has always had?*

A - *Nothing is ever either/or. It is always both, everything. Yes, both is involved here. There is an extra component now in the brain that is developing over the years. It lies in the grey area that they - meaning scientists and medical persons - do not understand. It has been developing, as has the rest of the body, the rest of the human condition. Yet, there is also more of an opening now in the human race for this type of communication to occur. People are not as wary of things they cannot see, things they do not understand, things they are learning to trust.*

Q - **Where do monkeys come from?**

A - From the sea as fish, from the leaves of trees, from the beach of sand, from the law of the land.

Q - **Are ESP cells or psychic ability inherited from the mitochondria of the maternal cells or is this ability coming from someplace else?**

A - In or out you ask?   Both is relevant. There must be a vehicle - as the human brain and mind is - for thought processes and evolution, technology, and science.
    There are DNA cells and also within some genes (which have not been discovered yet) you will see, as time goes on that, yes, the genes are most relevant in passing on the potential for this ability.   The ability is not always noticed and that comes from the outside sometimes.

Q - **Are the children being born today more psychically advanced?**

A - Of course.

Q - **Because the culture today is more receptive?**

A - It is because of evolution as a whole.   It is also because they have lived more past lives.

Q - Do all spirits have to evolve from animals to man to spirit, up the evolutionary ladder? If not, why is it said that all men are created equal?

A - Just in that theory alone there is a contradiction. If one must climb, as you say, a ladder of evolution, then no one is equal for one step at a time that must be. The circle becomes the equal for at any point on a circle you are equal with another. The question really seems to be that of growth, that of a step-by-step pattern of growth, and that not need be the case in some instances.

Q - What is a walk-in?

A - Walk-ins occur much less than human livings appear to believe. A change in such persons usually is their own soul finally listening to their own spirit and higher knowledge of the Light. Yet, walk - ins do occur, not frequently, but they do.

Q- Is a walk-in a spirit's own evolution or another spirit?

A - I may say what purpose do we think would be achieved by having one jump in in the middle of a life? For is this of the highest good? I may say that when you enter into soul from spirit, it is same soul learning different ways to jump.

Q - Could you explain what involution is?

A - Evolution, as I have said, is a changing, growing reality. Involution seems to just indicate stagnation. Whether in the form of going backwards, as it were, or staying where you are. There is a very strong concept of this involution among many of organized religion.

You're either going to go up and be with those of the Light or you're going to go down and be with those of the evil. This is a false distinction. This is a false reality. All that are growing are working toward the Light. There are souls who disconnect from spirit that may be an involution at this time, or stagnation. Yet that will be rectified so all really is evolution. There is only an illusion of the backward thinking process.

Q - Janith, did the world really end and when? And is the New Age a change in consciousness all over the world?

A - It depends on definition of "really." I may say that earth is existing as a planet but the persons on earth and the consciousness they hold was greatly beginning to change.

Q - Are we now coming into the evolutionary stage or the day of the Parabrahman as Prasad calls it?

A - You are there.

SOUL SENSE

---

*"A truth of soul is only
recognized when the person
knows of it's existence.
That's when we discover
our true self."*

                    JANITH

Many people speak of "the path" they follow on the journey to spiritual awakening. For me, it was more like a jungle overgrown with thorny unknowns. To carve my path, I had to chop through the heavy brush of different belief systems, philosophies, and concepts, with a machete sharper than reason.

Because I didn't follow any particular spiritual master, I had to lead my own safari. Most of what I learned was through books and personal experiences, and there were always too many questions that were left unanswered.

One of the greatest benefits of having a relationship with Janith is that I finally am able to ask those questions and receive answers that I can understand and accept. She's helped me through that brush of the unknown so that I can see my path more clearly. My hope is that her words will do the same for you.

The questions and answers in this chapter include a model of the anatomy of a soul and its connection to spirit, and the explanation of the dynamics of that interaction.

Q - What is the difference, if there is one, between soul and spirit?

A - A spirit soars, a soul discovers. A spirit is free, a soul is burdened. The difference between them is one of our plane and yours. It is one of what must remain an individual in order to touch down into physical body. A soul is a man's soul. We as spirits do not have a soul and that is the difference.

Q - How does one break away from the One to come into a physical body?

A - First the decision must be made as to what we are willing to use to grow next. If that decision becomes that of a physical body that we wish to learn in, then we, individually (which is a fragment of the Whole) must take on a soul, which is labeled then, a man's soul. In that soul is all the information that spirit will need before it touches down into physical body. Once that soul has entered physical body, its spirit is left with us to connect in dream, to connect in death, to connect in crisis.

Q - And it's that soul, Janith, that goes from one lifetime to another intact with the lessons we've learned?

A - Yes, oh yes. That soul is free to travel wherever it may since we are still connected with its spirit. Therefore, there is, as you would like to say, a silver cord, not only between soul and physical body, but between physical body, soul, and spirit.

Q - How is a spirit or a soul formed? How is a new spirit formed?

A - There is not a new spirit, yet there are new souls for they come from spirits who wish to enter physical body who may not have entered before. So you do have new souls that come from already existing spirits.

Q - So spirits are always One?

A - Yes.

Q - Why are new souls created?

A - New souls are created for many reasons.

    1 - Because old souls who have traveled their own long path to the gates of our land are done and may forever reside in the Light and help "others" as it were.

    2 - To inherit a part of the world that old souls may not; for there is no use for such a situation.

    3 - For the continuation of spirit life. You must not only assume that physical ones have to reproduce in order to keep their race alive. Spiritual reproduction is a way of making new souls.

Q - And when you come to earth, if you ever decide, you will become a new soul?

A - It is a new soul for it is the first soul of that spirit. Yet, depending upon how much knowledge that spirit has obtained through different means other than man's soul, is what information that soul will contain. So, it is not necessarily new, yet it is first.

Q - Can a spirit split into two souls or more than one soul at the same time?

A - This is rarely done unless a specific cause has been signified before entering. The only purpose of this is for faster growing knowledge. This must be obtained usually in identical twins for, other than that, it does not happen any quicker than each spirit taking each soul.

Q - Does a soul ever belong to two human livings?

A - This happens in very rare cases when a strong connection has been made. It happens quite frequently in these rare cases between mother and child in womb. A deal is made between soul and soul, which then enters into a unified soul, which enters into an agreement with two spirits and their connection of shared knowledge.

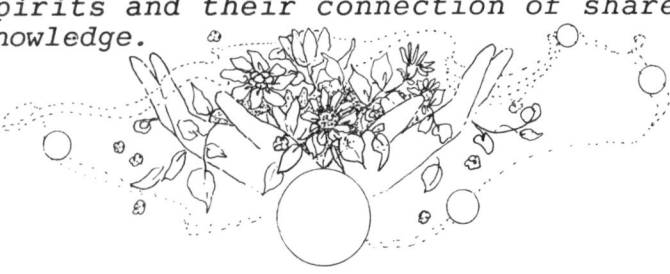

Q - Why would two different spirits, Janith, choose to share the same soul?

A - Two spirits have many reasons for trying to accomplish what can only be accomplished by this action.

Q - Would you please explain what occurs in this case?

A - I will speak of mother-child connection as it is one way of helping two spirits find out similar things on opposite sides of the learning situation. Let Janith see if we can make this clearer.
        Let us say that there is a geranium plant. Mother comes from one side, seeing this side of plant; child comes from other side of the same plant. They are together making whole concept that can bring back to two spirits abundant knowledge of a wholeness that cannot be seen from only one side of the geranium plant.

Q - Are earth twins created at the spirit level or at the soul level?

A - Different cases have been recorded. Identical twins most often come from the same spirit split into two souls to accomplish a faster learning process.

        Fraternal twins are of the One yet of different spirit entities that have decided on different choices for their soul's destiny.

Q - Can two or more souls occupy the same body?

A - This is done in some cases for there is a need of understanding on different levels in different ways. And this may be accomplished in this way.

Q - Is this what we on earth call multiple personality?

A - It may be, depending on how these souls decide to manifest in the three dimensional world.

Q - Is multiple personality that stems from early childhood sexual abuse caused by entity attachment?

A - I may say, "caused by," as seen as a manifestation on the physical level? Of course.

Q - Does thinning "I" shock allow this to happen? How?

A - You have said cause? Thinning "I" shock is more cause. The outward show of many personalities is exactly that. Psychology makes this quite complicated; for when there is more than one speaking, there is more than one there.

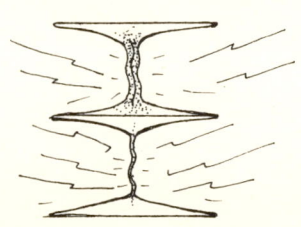

Q - Would depossession be a treatment in this case?

A - I do not feel it is possession in the sense of "evil." I feel it is only lost souls looking for a home and not being directed toward the Light. I may say that an "unattachment" program might be helpful.

Q - Can the soul return to spirit before the body dies?

A - This is what happens in every case; for the body does not die until soul is connected again with spirit.

Q - How far in advance can that be?

A - Minutes.

Q - Where does the soul go when we die?

A - We, meaning physical body? The death of the physical body then releases the soul back to the spirit for it is no longer needed to occupy an individual space in the universe. So it then becomes absorbed back into that spirit which was once connected, as one, with that soul at the beginning.

Q - Why are there more people on earth now?

A - There are.more people on earth now, because the older souls are not learning as quickly as ones used to, because of technology which has slowed spiritual growth considerably. New souls keep coming, for this is right, for reasons just given. Therefore, "more" inhabit the earth at this point in illusion time.

Q - What is the ultimate goal of a soul?

A - To become one with the Light. It is so wonderful, this Light, there could never be words to describe it.

Q - After becoming one with the Light, what happens?

A - All who are with The Light are of God and Joy. This is the end to our means.

Q - Does a soul ever have an enemy?

A - Depending on definition used. There are no victims. There are no enemies, in reality, for it is a different definition we speak of than that of traditional society on earth says it is. Enemy is a valuable friend. Therefore yes, on all levels of physical mind, emotion and spirit, enemies do exist, for they remain a catalyst for learning.

Q - Is there any such a thing as a spirit enemy?

A - There is, as you can see it now from a soul level, spirit enemies. They do exist, for it is only our definition of enemy that is different.
Enemy could be one of the greatest tools of learning. Enemy seen as that could help so much in growing process, for it is steps to overcome in order for the soul to take on and learn the process for which it came.

Q - At what point do we each recognize our true self?

A - A truth of soul is only recognized when the person knows of its (the soul's) existence. At this point, it takes on its own body and therein begins the inward workout.

Q - Janith, what is contained in the soul? Does the soul have a mind? Is it rational or irrational and if it is a rational soul, what does the soul-mind base it's logic on?

A - Very good recognition of soul first being of another sort than incorporating into physical. This is a very good way to translate meaning. Soul, yes, is an entity of and in itself and it does contain all attributes of what we see in physical. Rational? As rational as that soul's purpose needs to be. Irrational? The same. Its logic is based on knowledge that it is aware of. This is an important point to remember, for that is why awareness needs to be heightened.

Q - Is there such a thing as a soul body? Does it have special centers?

A - Of course. Five.

Q - Could you please tell us what the five centers in the soul body are and what their purpose is?

A - Two located in hands represent healing manifestations of the plane of consciousness which is of highest healing power. These two centers contain all aspects of All in different formation in different levels of consciousness.

The top formation signifies what we see as soul mind, soul knowledge, soul comprehension.

The middle is of soul emotion, soul pleasure, soul pain and soul purpose.

The third remains on a grounding level, remains an individual nature, and also contains blueprint of information from spirit.

Q - Are there corresponding colors for soul centers?

A - Top in soul mind is yellow. Hands, one green and one orange, for in their combination they give out a ray of red which is repellent so that many of the ills are not absorbed into soul.

Middle is one of varied colors, depending on emotion of soul at the time. That does change.

Bottom may be seen as brown, orange, or red, depending on the level of remembrance of soul.

Q - And what is the L connection in the middle?

A - Body connection to soul as well as soul connection to spirit.

Q - What is contained in the bottom of the feet?

A - Those are various pressure points in locating different knowledge on soul level.

Q - What purpose does the grounding energy center serve in the soul, and what kind of information is contained in the blueprint of the soul?

A - This center serves as a conception process. This is the first center which is formed in order to touch down into soul. It is, as you might see, the first soul cell of the body. It is the first soul cell of the mind. It also contains what lessons you have already accomplished, what lessons are needed, and what lessons you hope to learn, so that soul may not forget that information. Blueprint of soul level may be changed. This is also a center of choice.

Q - Is memory stored in the top, middle
or ground centers of the soul?
A - Top.

Q - So that's in the rational soul mind?

A - We may say, if the connection is not
very great with middle, bottom, top
centers, look how simple it might be for
lower center to make different choice
than memory center on top...

Q - Does a soul have future vision?

A - Of course. You have asked about
psychic. That is future vision of soul.

Q - Do colors have a corresponding
emotion on a human level?

A - This would be seen in many different
variables, for depending upon human
experience would make meaning of color
different.

Q - Is the soul body contained within the
physical body or does it emanate from the
physical body as does a magnetic field or
aura?

A - I do not wish this soul body
described or associated with
aura/magnetic field. It is quite
different. Yet, I may say, of course
its origin is within. Yet, it is quite
bigger than physical so it would be seen
from outside vision as well.

Q - A soul body can be seen then?

A - Of course.

Q - By clairvoyants?

A - Well, I may say that anyone who wishes to see it can see it; it is quite obvious so that it spills. Do you know that this is why Indians made shields? Everyone has one, yet they needed a more apparent vision. Soul body will tell you all about a person.

Q - How can one develop the ability to see soul?

A - Develop? I wish to say rather "look for."

Q - When one reads Janith, does information reach soul mind memory and how is it retained?

A - It reaches soul mind and is retained in soul memory.

Q - When one's physical mind feels shut down, is it a soul's awareness that tells one that physical mind is shut down?

A - It is soul's rational mind, not its awareness. When I speak of awareness, I am speaking of maybe what you call enlightenment. That is much more than a rational mind of a soul.

Q - Does spirit have a mind?   And can you tell us what the basis of that is?

A - The basis of spirit mind is All.

Q - Are past life memories contained in the soul memory?

A - Past life memories are contained in soul blueprint, if they are not resolved. For they are truly meant to be worked on in the NOW life.

Q - Does an attack like rape imprint on soul memory or soul blueprint?

A - I may say that it is not so easy to find blueprint of another.   It is not so easy to mix blueprint of another.   Yet, it is quite easy to retain this on soul memory.   Also too, if situation involves child, compassion of the child lets in a mixing of that soul/spirit connection.

Q - Does rape imprint only on soul memory or also on spirit blueprint and soul/spirit connection?

A - It is obviously contained in soul memory, but blueprint is almost more like picture.   Memory is more like "knowing" storage.   Blueprint fades.

Q - A soul blueprint can fade?

A - If we are not constantly penciling in.

Q - That sounds awful.

A - No, it is not awful. It is of changing, growing and Light. It is not awful. I must say I must speak something for it was not asked, for I do not think the human living mind knows of this. There are three different types of blueprints - only.

Q - Could you please tell us what they are?

A - Of course. One is butterfly blueprint; another is frog blueprint; another is turtle blueprint.

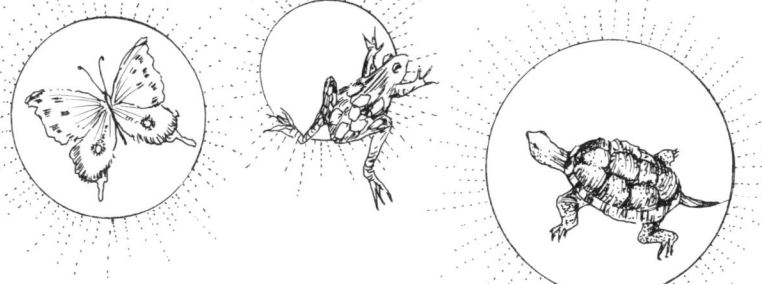

Q - Do you want to tell us what they mean?

A - Of course. Correlation? Turtle blueprint is one of what you see in the material world as Wall Street businessman. Very slow in changing consciousness along its way.

Frog consciousness blueprint, on other hand, hops from one transformation to another and it is not quite an easy transformation. It is quite upsetting.

Butterfly transcends. Many of the spiritual high leaders have butterfly blueprints.

Q - So each spirit gives a soul one of these three blueprints?

A - Like a stamp. Like a stamp of approval.

Q - What information should we be penciling into our spirit blueprint to keep it from fading?

A - Penciling in, as sketching in, every moment of experience learned.

Q - Janith, can one change a turtle or a frog blueprint to a butterfly blueprint?

A - Why would they wish to?

Q - Can frogs and turtles become enlightened or only butterflies?

A - All these limitations! Each and every blueprint will become enlightened. Depending on how is how blueprint works. Selective enlightenment? Such another funny concept.

Q - Where is all the other information stored that is not in blueprint?

A - Soul memory. Soul mind. Depending on what is appropriate.

Q - Does the sun have an effect on people's soul emotions?

A - Of course. I may say that if the soul is not finding enough light of its own, the sun may do this for it. This will bring about a high vibrational change of love, joy, pleasure. I may say that if Light is found from within, you may live in a tunnel.

Q - Why does the soul sometimes go on "Red Alert." What is the danger?

A - The soul, as I have said before, brings together past and future and brings it into present situation. This is where the danger red alert signs come from, for it cannot distinguish of time. It is only a recognition of a danger in previous life, maybe; in future life, maybe. It is obstacle recognition. Yet, it is not seen with rational mind for it does not exclude the present communication from its fears.

Q - Would a soul recognize another person's stagnant soul, or their own, and interpret it or perceive it as evil or negative?

A - A soul would send out a red alert but it would have to be interpreted through rational mind of physical to be interpreted as evil. Soul mind does not have judgements in the same way as does physical mind. So a soul will recognize, if developed, another soul and the condition of that soul as you would recognize a physical condition of another, or yourself, depending on how in tune you are with that person and with your own physical body.

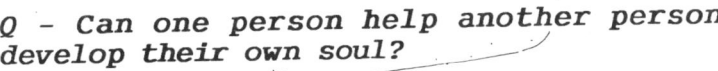

Q - Can one person help another person develop their own soul?

A - This is as silly as asking if you may grow another's hair.

Q - What is the "I" that we all feel?

A - The "I" is that place that connects spirit and soul. For without spirit connection, soul would be empty and that would leave a very hard physical body, a very hard mind, a very hard person.

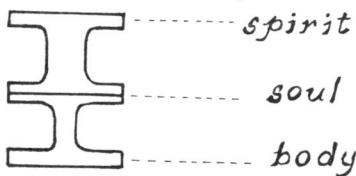

Q - What is the result of an empty soul? What form does it take on earth that we would recognize?

A - An empty soul would be seen through (I's) and eyes. It is not hard to see these ones who have no connection to spirit for they remain as lifeless as if their body had died. Which may be the case in some other instances.

Q - If soul is born of spirit, how can a soul ever lose its connection to the spirit?

A - Again, once soul has been decided on, and formulated, and brought down into body, then that soul has free choice. In that free choice may be a decision to disconnect from their higher self, their spirit knowledge, for it may be counterproductive to what they feel they should be doing on this earth at this time.

Q - Why is there so much hurt on an emotional and psychic level in the individual victim of sexual child abuse?

A - These children are very highly evolved souls and they know of the sad condition of the "abuser," as it were. They feel sorrow on an emotional level for the problems they are witnessing between a soul/spirit connection and they see the desperateness of that person who comes to them for comfort, to share in their connection with their spirit. It is sort of not only an attack on the physical, it is an attack on the greatest I - that special connection between that spirit and its soul. That is affected greatly with this kind of occurrence.

Q - Is there such a thing as spiritual psychosis or spiritual shock?

A - No. There is such a thing as soul/spirit shock. "I" shock.

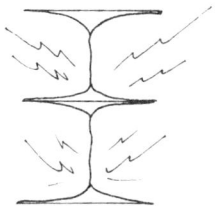

Q - What can that come from?

A - Many, many, many things. I may say that one of these things is exactly what we may call rape.

Q - How does "I" shock manifest itself?

A - Thinning.

Q - What is the purpose of thinning, Janith? Usually these reactions are compensatory, so why would it thin in "I" shock?

A - I may say that it thins <u>with</u> shock. "I" shock is consistent with <u>what</u> human livings know as grief response. This is seen in all loss, so it is not surprising that when something is taken - as is taken in rape - that you have thinning "I" shock.

Q - Can a spiritual counselor help with thinning "I" shock? How?

A - I may say that first they must acknowledge that this one has been taken of, not only in physical/soul but also in soul/spirit.
      Then, by giving unconditional love. And by helping strengthen soul/spirit connection from bottom up, which begins with soul emotion releasing. Then the work must be done in rebuilding and thickening.
      Help with "I" shock must be done by spiritual counselors, obviously, for other therapies do not even consider such a thing to be. So how can they help fix?

Q - Does one have to experience some kind of thinning "I" shock before a transformation can occur?

A - Have to? Never. I may also say that it is usually accomplished in this way; for rational mind stands so much in the way of transformation that it is quite much easier in this way.

Q - What happens to the soul/spirit connection during a convulsion or seizure?

A - It becomes wide. It becomes encompassing. It becomes the place where that person lives, as it were, in that time of seizure.

Q - What happens to the soul/body connection during seizure, Janith?

A - Body may be said to be dormant at this time for soul has entered into maybe like the middle plane of that place, of that connection. So body is doing whatever body does when soul does not occupy a great majority of it.

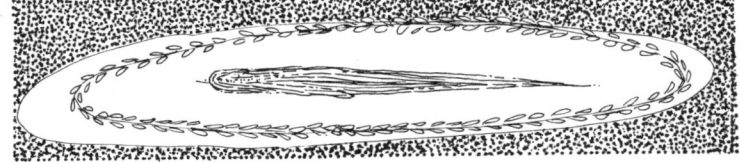

Q - Could you then explain why epilepsy and possession have been confused or seen as the same thing?

A - It is always easier for rational mind to make up reasons why something looks the way it does. Perceptions are funny things. They could have a number of explanations for one reality that is in actuality happening. A feeling that I think human livings get is that the body is not completely occupied by that person, therefore it must be open to, as rational mind says, anything that may be around that wants to occupy this so called empty or partially empty physical body.

Q - Is that true? Can anything enter and is it empty?

A - As I said before, soul and spirit are coming close and wide and great in that connection whereas body is somewhat dormant. Yet, it still is claimed. It still is not given up. It still is not offered. And without the offering, it cannot be taken because it is not something that is coming from fear or allowance. It is coming from something that is happening between that soul and its spirit. That remains sacred, that remains something that is right and it would not be of the Light to have this dormant body occupied without permission or fear as an inducer.

Q - Could you please tell us what anesthesia does to the connections between spirit/soul and soul/body?

A - It is much the same as a sleeping human. For it is only an induced consciousness that may be achieved in sleep yet usually isn't. It may be seen as out of body and when out of body, depending on intention, and depending on growth, is where you will reside in spirit/soul connection during this length of time.

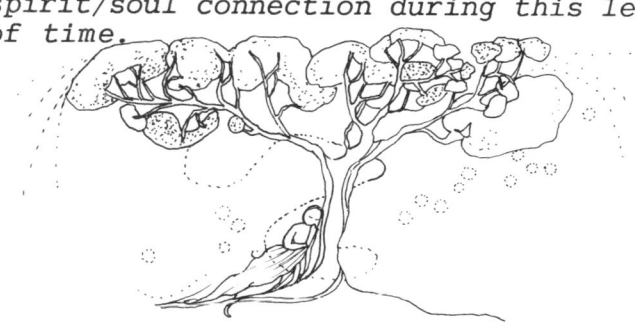

Q - It seems that high intensity stimulation during deep coma or autism elicits a positive response and is helpful. Is this so?

A - It is seen to be the case, so yes, it is the case - in some instances. Also as I have explained in seizure, also in autism, also in coma, where body does not look fully occupied, you must bring back body knowledge to body. You must bring back spirit/soul connection to body. One attempt may be at overstimulation of body to make it bigger than it remains in that soul's atmosphere.

Q - And another?

A - Another will take so much longer. Another is, as I said before, a very high thought process that will encompass this type of reaction to a soul/spirit connection and nurture it. And recognize it as only that and therefore there will be no fear, there will be no waiting, as it were, for someone to return, for they have not really left.

Q - How are each of us connected to the others?

A - We are all fragments in the universe of God, all pieces of the puzzle. God is the whole puzzle, the whole universe. We are but threads which weave the fabric of One. If one thread breaks the whole fabric has a hole in it.

Q - When all souls are of The Light, what then?

A - Then we have a whole New World. One that can only be imagined in fairy tales right now. But believe me it will be a "happily ever after" story.

BRIDGES BETWEEN SOUL AND SPIRIT

"Any interaction between
two beings, three beings,
four beings....gives different
sights, different worlds,
different visions. And in that
interplay, different ideas and
different realms."

JANITH

Janith tells us that it is now a time in our world of great growth and change. In order to help quicken the pace of our evolution, we are being asked to look within ourselves for our strength, for our inner guides, for our God. And we are being offered help from other more highly-evolved realms.

But, it is up to us to discriminate between those communications that are truly helpful and those that are not; whether they come from without or within. Because we don't really know the territory, we asked Janith to help us with some guidelines. In order to traverse the territory safely and most effectively, we needed more knowledge about the subtle worlds.

In this chapter we've included information on channeling and other methods of spirit guidance as well as questions and answers on how to avoid the pitfalls of the lower worlds of consciousness.

Q - How do you wish us to refer to you?

A - Depending on who we speak to. I feel that High Spirit of Creative Communications of the Specialist kind will be fine. Or just Angel.

Q - Janith, could you give us a definition of channeling?

A - I may say that channeling in the highest form is a blessed communication, a gift from God, The One, The All-Knowledge. A gift of allowing a communication to be between two realms of spirit and soul/spirit. Do you know that channeling occurs on many levels?

Q - Can you give us some information on the different levels of channeling?

A - Channeling, as the most important concept, is a gift, so this is not something that can be looked after, desired after, wanted after. It must be given to.

I am now speaking of channeling as in our communication, for this is truly where the word should be used, in the form of a communication between two realms.

Channeling in the way that human livings seem to have used it, are using it, will be using it, is quite different. Channeling of the Light, allowing the Light to flow freely through one's soul, is quite good. But it must remain in all areas. If we become stagnant in only one seeked-after area, then this becomes not of the Light, so we are not speaking of a true channeling experience.

Q - Janith, can anyone channel?

A - Anyone who has decided to come down as such and who has been given the gift. For it seems to me a gift, not a decision of a soul, of a person, of a human living, but a decision, a gift, from God.

Q - What's the difference between channeling and schizophrenia?

A - Oh my goodness! Janith as an aspect of a psychosis? Quite a funny idea. I may say that schizophrenics have come to earth to show different sights to others, to expand visions, and so has Janith. Yet, I feel this aspect, in this way, is quite more respectful of the human living; their mind, their emotional state, soul/spirit.
     For it is not only one consciousness in this body, it is two when I am here, so it could be considered schizophrenic (if we wish to call it this); yet, I may say, this has quite a different purpose on earth. Channeling has come in many different guises on your plane, yet channeling of Light, channeling of Love, is quite different from schizophrenia.

Q - How many true channels of Light are there Janith? And in what way do they channel?

A - I may say 23. Yet, I can only speak of what I, Janith, consider true channeling of Light, and that is in a communications form.

Q - Is there a difference between channeling and trance channeling?

A - Of course. Vibrational difference is of the highest importance.

Q - Trance channeling is of a higher vibration?

A - I need to speak more in specifics. For trance channeling is quite different from trance medium. Trance channeling would be of only spirits coming from Core Group of non-incarnational type.

Q - Those spirits who have never been in incarnation have a higher vibration, Janith?

A - This is quite obvious, for one must lower vibration to come into physicality, and this is always an imprint on soul/spirit.

Q - And those channeling high spirits who have been in incarnation are trance mediums?

A - Of course.

Q - How long is the apprenticeship for a medium?

A - As long as it takes each individual living to be able to accept truth from other planes without the confusion of the ego. Once one can hear and accept with no involvement from lower selves, or lower bodies, then one will be an absolute truthful healer and medium.

Q - Could you please explain some uses of a trance medium for the highest good?

A - I may say of trance mediums, this can be of use in a number of healing ways. First, they are quite a validation for ones who do not believe in other realms at this time. Also, they can provide ears for ones who cannot hear on their own.

Q - Is the ability to help heal as a trance medium a gift, or can anyone acquire it with practice and commitment?

A - Trance medium is the ultimate goal of all who live. For if they can communicate with other realms, it would be quite helpful for each and everyone to learn from. Yet, I am not necessarily speaking of vocal; they do not have to whisper out what they hear.

Q - What are the real dangers for mediums?

A - There is never danger when one resides in the Light. God protects His/Her own. Of this, have no worry. No "real" problems of any kind comes from the highest level to those who are not prepared sufficiently.

Q - Are there positive and negative polarities of spirit? And how can we as human beings recognize the differences?

A - Positive and negative exists on all levels of consciousness. I do not feel you need to decipher. I feel you need to feel. Positive vibrational energy feels quite different from negative.

Q - How can one tell, Janith, if the spirit or entity one is channeling is higher than one's higher self and separate from it?

A - First, I must qualify my answer. One must be quite on the spiritual path before one should even attempt such an experience. If it is not given to, it is being seeked after, and the gift is maybe not there for them to have. Yet, I may say, the experience will show them the difference.

Q - What is the difference between using trance channeling or direct voice? Would that be vibrational as well?

A - Absolutely. I may say trance channeling may only occur with highest vibrational spirit energy. Direct voice may be used in almost any communication.

Q - Can you please tell us, Janith, how one would know if one is channeling one's own higher self or another spirit?

A - Is asking not good enough?

Q - Would another spirit always be truthful?

A - Well, of course, I may say, the first question is, "Are you of The Light?" Yet, the second question must be, "Who art thou?"

Q - Can we have some guidelines to distinguish between the quality of the messages and to distinguish between the validity of the spirits themselves?

A - Human minds, human souls are capable of good judgement. Are capable of interpreting the spiritual on not only an instinctual level, an intuitive level, but also on a rational level. And I feel it is quite important to look with your mind, not only your mind's eye, at these answers, at these communications. Are they causing harm? Do they interrupt with destiny? Are they taking from more than they are giving to? Basically, it is much the same as a very good human relationship, a very giving relationship, a very comfortable relationship. Also, is it a growing relationship? This must remain the most important test, if you will, of a channel spirit communication relationship. For if does not allow or precipitate growth, then it is and does become the worst form of stagnation which remains not good.

Q - Is there a difference between the depth of channeling that is indicated by a channel's open or closed eyes?

A - It is an individual question at this point. It remains unimportant, yet, if that channel is unable to have a closed mind's eye with physical eyes open, then closed physical eyes must be accomplished. If it is possible, though, to keep open eyes, this would be all right. It doesn't remain better. However that channel feels he/she is able to transmit the closer, more accurate, truthful, information, is fine.

Q - Can higher spirits get corrupt after they experience physicality for a while? Is that a legitimate concern?

A - A legitimate concern of mine? I know this not to be so. It is a funny concept to me to consider that I am not happy where I am. I am offering help. I am here to learn. Yet, I am not here to take. If ever our relationship becomes taking, I wish to dissolve it. And I wish for you to help dissolve it.

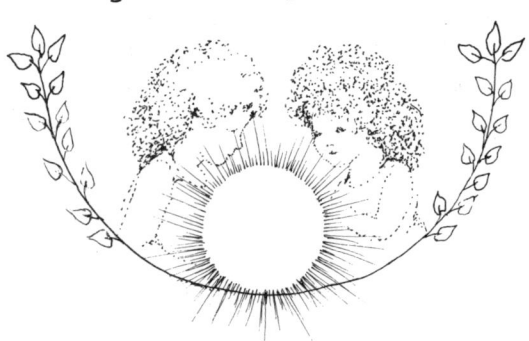

Q - Janith, could you please explain how we, as human beings, can discriminate between earthbound souls who wish to inhabit a human body for their own sensual pleasure, and higher spirits who wish to trance channel in order to help the All in their clearer understanding of the One?

A - As I have said before, this is an experience of personal understanding. I think human livings are evolved enough to <u>feel</u> the difference.

Masters of Darkness are not of the Light, for they do not see the Light at this time. They do not know of the Light in all its workings. So to be able to fool a human living that completely seems to be not a probability. There would be certain markers, if you will, certain differences in philosophy, different feelings. It is quite rare to have a total possession, as you would like to call it, by an earthbound soul. They cause a lot of trouble; they are very aggravating when they're not seen to be what they are. Yet, the possession of a human living is quite rare.

Q - Janith, could you please tell us who Masters of Darkness are?

A - I suppose the easiest correlation for human livings would be fallen angels.

Q - Do they get stuck there then, or is it a decision?

A - I may say that they wish to be exactly where they lie.

Q - Can Masters of Darkness have souls on earth as well?

A - All from the other side of the Light may not take on a soul, as such, from birth. Yet, they may encompass another's soul, from the Light, which must give an allowance of this truth.

Q - In the larger sense of things, are Masters of Darkness also part of the Light? As long as God is All?

A - They are what may be seen as polarities. Yet, I may say, there is a different realm that these ones exist on that is not of the Light, is not of the Rays, is not of the One.

Q - Could you tell us the difference between Masters of Illusion and earthbound souls?

A - Earthbound souls have been in incarnation.

Q - Could you tell us, Janith, where earthbound entities exist and how they play their games?

A - They exist on the same level as the physical. They are here; they are around; they are always around. If they were higher they couldn't come into physical.

Q - Do earthbound souls still maintain spirit connections?

A - Rarely.

Q - In what cases do they?

A - In cases of a temporary detainment, for maybe they have promised something to physical ones, maybe they are being stuck by physical ones' grieving, or they may be in a temporary setback, as it were. Yet, there are others who intentionally break this connection for they do not wish to leave physical plane.   It meant too much.

Q - Are Masters of Darkness negative spirits?

A - Fallen.

Q - What is the difference between negative spirits and Masters of Darkness?

A - Ah!   One has bad attitude, the other is evil.

Q - Can Masters of Darkness, earthbound souls, or negative spirits come through and channel?

A - Masters of Darkness do not care of knowledgeable allowance.   So, if there is a want for a channeling experience and it has not been given as a gift from God, it may be given from somewhere else.

Q - What protections can we use to assure that we're getting only our higher spirits?

A - There are no specifics other than the purple and illuminescent I have spoken of. Yet, I may say, that intention to be guided only by those who are for your highest good would be the greatest protection of all.

Q - Janith, how does one not allow an earthbound soul or a Master of Darkness to enter if they do not care of knowledgeable allowance? How can one be sure never to allow it?

A - The most efficient way is never allowing yourself to be fooled. How can one do this? Know thyself and know thy God.

Q - Are there any specific entities that we would need information to invalidate? Any entities at this time that we, as a whole, should be wary of?

A - I don't know whether human livings at this point on earth should not be wary of many things. I think it is not of the good to give energy of any type to these ones of darkness. It's hard for me to make you understand how "see through" these Masters of Darkness are. There is no question that they are not speaking from a place within the Light. It is not a question of whether we know the difference or not. It remains an individual knowledge of making that decision based on one's life experience.

Q - Could you explain what they call the seduction of the spirit entity? How does it take hold of a human being and why?

A - There are certain human livings who have only evolved to a certain point. You would see this as human livings who would put themselves in a situation of abuse by either physical or spirit. And why? Some feel they deserve this type of punishment, if you will. Some can't see these games. Yes, there are games of seduction but they're not very good games, they're very "see through" games. And once recognized for what they are, their power is gone. For the entire seduction remains an illusion and that is how not to let yourself be, as some like to say, a "victim." I don't consider any such beings as "victims" on earth. That is an illusion. The power of illusion comes from you as a human living. You have control, you can see with open eyes. There is fear that precipitates a lot of this. And that is really the tool that these masters play with. If that fear does not exist, then they don't have the tools to cause the damage.

Q - Can you please tell us the difference between a spirit and an entity?

A - The difference in the way that human livings use the words? I feel language is quite important, so we will say: entity is a lower vibrational spirit.

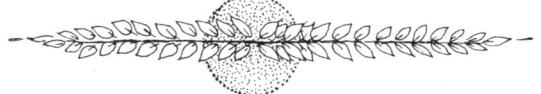

Q – Janith, what is death – not of the physical? And how can this be prevented?

A – Oh, soul death is what I speak of. When one gives over a soul, that is giving away a piece of spirit, a piece of a gift from God. Would you do such a thing?

Q – And one can never get it back?

A – Once a piece is gone, where do you get it back from? You would not want that back once that side of the universe has had its part in it.

Q – How can this be prevented?

A – I may say we must get back to ground level with human livings and that is – to know thyself and to know thy God. Then all shall remain right.

Q – Are physical-damage problems which occur in a house indications of the presence of earthbound souls?

A – It is indication of obstruction. I may say that earthbound souls have ways of not wanting people in their space.

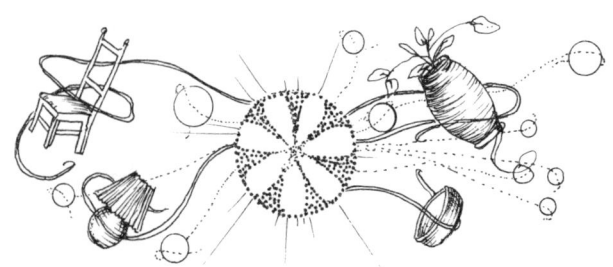

Q - How can one teach psychic self defense and not give energies to negative reality?

A - The beginning place of this is to know that the highest good and the most encompassing Light is the most effective. I may also say, if we are doing our own action and not doing a response to an initiated action then we are in the Light.

Q - What do you feel about depossessions? Who should do them and why do they occur, what purpose could this serve?

A - How does Janith feel about depossession? Quite well. I feel it would occur without help from outside people; yet, there have been ones sent down to accelerate this process. Possession occurs because of a free will of man, of man's initial curiosity, non-belief, and invalidation of spirit in either of its forms.

Q - Why are we sent guides?

A - Guides, both human and spirit, are helpers, not teachers. The best teacher is called Life. We are here to help you learn what is being taught. For ones who will not listen to us, we send human helpers to do the same work.

Q - People have a very big problem with energy levels. We're tired so much of the time. How can this be helped?

A - By each and every one connecting with guides, with their highest self, with their highest potentials. For in this interaction there should be an energizing situation occurring. It would not take more than a couple of minutes to completely recharge.

Q - Should that be asked for or is that a natural outcome of connecting with the guides?

A - Some need to be asked, some don't. I have spoken of vibration and this depends on the level of vibration of spirit involved. Couldn't hurt to ask.

Q - How can we transmit the reality of your words to others on this plane?

A - They must hear, they must feel, they must see, our reality. Through actual physical being with people and letting them hear our words as they are spoken - for the vibration will become apparent.
Or meditation within their own centers may prove to be a way. There will be people who our words will touch who would not have been open, would not have been growing, without them.

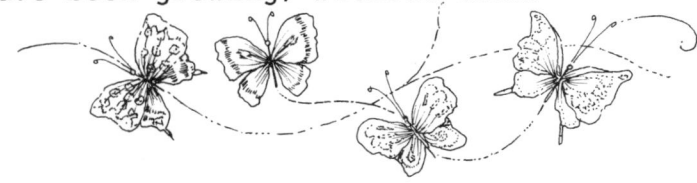

Q - Janith, can you share with us some of what you've learned from the beginning of our communication?

A - I have learned many things with our communication. I have observed many of the fears of man's soul, many of the truths, many of the insights, which is very interesting for me to see. I can also see how my words are put to practical use. How they are put to use in their interpretation of soul, and this I would not know in another way.

Q - Can you read human livings minds all of the time?

A - I may read, if you will, a human living's mind if it is of my purpose and of the purpose of that human living. So, yes must be the answer. All of the time is a strange concept for me.

Q - Can a spirit be in incarnation and still a guide at the spirit level?

A - Of course. This goes on many times in dream state, for when asleep your spirit may choose to communicate with others and see and solve problems and guide.

Q - At this point in time are you a guide for anyone else or channeling through anyone else?

A - I hope I am a guide for many, yet I am not channeling at this time through any other human living.

Q - Can you tell us if you're part of the Circle of Wisdom?

A - Oh! My my, I certainly hope so.

Q - Can you give us some Laws of Manifestation Janith, to be used for only the highest good of All?

A - Of course,we may start with three. Most important is:
    1 - Analyze your want. For one must be very careful with this manifestation ability empowerment. It could be quite a disharmonizing experience if not done well from beginning. Be Sure.

    2 - I feel would be visualization. Yet from a soul "I," from a soul center. Not from mind's eye.

    3 - One must exist as if one is living within that situation and know that you are calling. And this is what will be there.

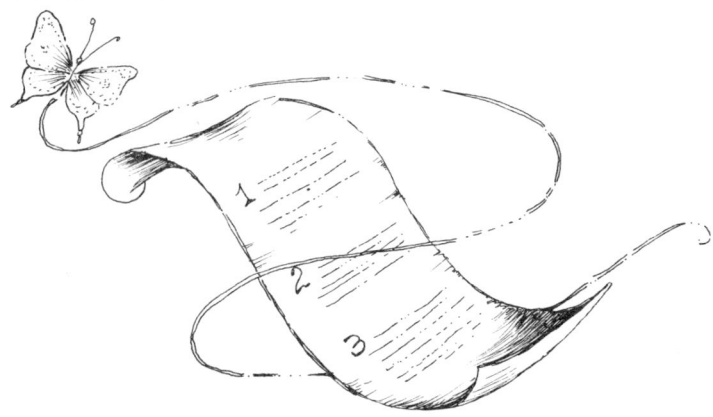

Q - There are many entities appearing
through channels. It seems as though our
filtering systems are becoming thin so
this may occur. How does a student
determine the appropriate channel to
learn from? Or spirit to learn from?

A - I must beg to differ that it has not
so much to do with a filtering system, as
you would call it, but a receptiveness
that has always been there. Filtering
implies allowing something to infiltrate
or come through a screen, as it were. I
seem to think that the open receptiveness
of human livings is much greater than
ever before. It is time now. That
becomes the reason why in everything, in
every question, no matter what.
    A student's problem? Well, this
seems to be an individual choice, of
individual acknowledgement of what
lessons are needed to be learned, of what
path that student seems to be following
at this point in time.

Q - If the consciousness that we have
labelled Janith communicates with the
consciousness that we call Teri, and is a
separate stream of consciousness out of
the main, how is it of the highest good?

A - We are only one voice that has been
singled out as to make it more
comfortable for the human mind to
understand. Teri must be in contact with
specific names, relations, guides,
because it is too hard for her to
understand a crowd. The human mind does
not absorb as well as other forms of
consciousness do. We are very much the
One, the All Knowledge. The difference
is made on your plane not ours.

Q - If people don't experience for themselves the knowledge that you are giving us, what use does it have in that person's life?

A - It is use for all who hear our words for that becomes part of their experience.

Q - Janith, what is the practical value of our communication?

A - If it becomes a philosphy of soul, then its practical use becomes apparent. If it is only a philosophy of mind then daily use doesn't necessarily become involved. When one absorbs this type of philosophy, one lives it. If the human race sees different visions, hears different words, sees more than they are seeing now, that is all we can hope at this point. Its practical use will be seen through evolution.

Q - It seems as if people who know of your reality would already know many of the concepts that you talk about. And the people who don't know your reality exists would have no use for this material. Is this so?

A - We may have negated that this material has been said before. I don't believe it has been. In a different way, in a different life, in a different form, maybe. Yet, the words we deliver and the way we deliver them will become a unique one; a different and growing experience for those who do believe in other realities. And for those who don't, they are not ready and that is fine.

Q - Is it correct, for the highest good, to teach others to channel?

A - Can you teach a gift?

Q - Are you feeling any more inclined to come to earth since you know us?

A - I wish for none to take this as an insult, but, I may say, no, Janith has quite a comfortable area of space in the Light and will remain so. For I can be of great help here and I can see many things Janith has not said as of this time, has not done at this time. We will spend many years together and this is quite enough of Janith's exposure to earth plane.

WHOLE - I - NESS

"I am a seeker of Truth;
I am a giver of Love."

JANITH

Whenever we step into unknown territory, it helps to be able to map that ground with concepts we already know. Therefore, when we began communicating with Janith, we asked questions about religions and belief systems that were already accepted. Good spirit communication should be consistent with the great body of mystical writings we already have, even as it takes us a little farther into our own understanding. Of course, Janith's did.

This chapter is about rediscovering many of the basic truths that have run throughout some of the major religions and integrating them with concepts of the new spirituality which focus on the spirit or God spark within. It's about taking that which is truly holy and honoring it within ourselves and each other. It's about balancing our spiritual, soul, emotional, and physical aspects in order to become whole, more evolved human beings.

Q - What is the purpose of religion?

A - To help human livings on their first steps. This is a good beginning when they are not ready for more. When they are, no organized religions need be because all will know from within and no words will be needed, no sermons on the mount (pulpit). Nothing but love, trust, God, The One.

Q - Who was Jesus?

A - Jesus was a friend to all mankind. A good man who knew his own life's plan from start to finish, way past his time of birth. As a young child, he knew he was special and he knew this so well, that others knew the same. It was true. He was a true son of God, but he most assuredly wasn't the only.

People focus on this man as if he were one to be idolized. But if each could try to copy his life in his awareness, this would be the true worshiper.

It is not God's will to look at another and idolize. It is God's will to look at another and learn to be that idol himself. Each man has the same capability as Jesus or Solomon.

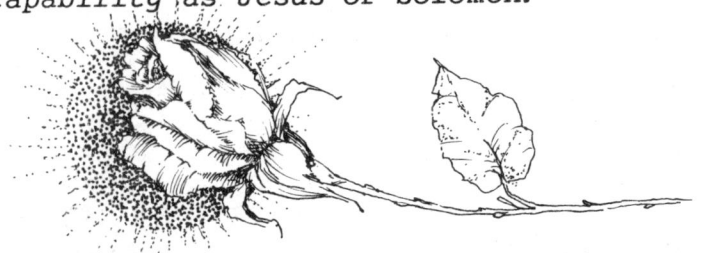

Q - Do we each get to play a different part as each of the disciples in each life? And Christ and Judas too?

A - I may say that each and every one of human livings have played and are playing, will play, every part that ever existed. Not only of disciples, symbolically, but of everything.

Q - When the bible, in ST. John, says it's not every spirit you can trust, is that true? Are there spirits who can't be trusted to be true?

A - There are spirits who feel they are being true, yet they are not total truthful healers so they need practice. And I must say that it would be not of the highest good to use or communicate with these ones for a higher understanding of absolute truth. For they do not have one.

Q - What is the Adam and Eve story symbolic of?

A - This is a nice question. Adam represents good. Eve represents evil. By definition I have already given you, good is growth; bad stunts growth which constitutes evil. Eve gave in and took something God did not want her to, metaphorically, followed the wrong path. She then tried to steer her brother into going away from his life's mission also. There can be no bigger "sin" than to ignore life's plans once made. That is why it is called "original sin." From this original sin come all other wrongs in life.

Q - Are there correlations in your system for the Heaven, Purgatory and Hell of religions? Can you tell us what they are and explain a little about them?

A - Heaven is what you see as the Core Group. I may say Heaven is the middle of our Ray system: the circular motion, the counseling, advising, guiding factor of the universe.

I may say that Purgatory is a decision place. It is quite different from pay-back place, from a waiting for no reason place. It is decision place. A stopover.

Also, Hell is a choice. It is free will. It is not of flames, but of self-judgement, self-persecution, of Fear. One may wind up in a hellish space for a little while, yet ones of Light will not let this continue.

Q - Is there a correlation between celibacy and the spiritual life?

A - Celibacy is a man made concept. It has nothing to do with the One, the All-Knowledge, except for the fact that these "men of God" cannot become spiritual when still allowing for physical intimacy. This becomes their problem. For it is not right to make oneself "higher" than anyone else. True love for another is an ultimate goal for all spiritual leaders. Negating the sexual negates a part, which then doesn't become total love, only partial love, for it is not loving the whole. No need for such an act, for they are no closer to the Light from such a situation.

Q - Could you please tell us what you feel about the religious practice of communion?

A - As in religious communion? I feel as if this communion is an internal happening within the soul in its revelation and connection with God, The Light: internally finding a glowing space within one's self, a Christ consciousness. To be given something external that we wish to intake seems quite unnecessary.

Q - Who was the Buddha?

A - The Buddha. A man of age, a man of wisdom, yet a man. He was one of enlightened truths that tried to come to terms in his world with what he saw as unjust, as unfair, as reality. Buddha was a man of compassion and that's what he should be remembered as for he was truly the most enlightened one who has ever touched down on the earth.

Q - Could you tell me what the purpose of surrendering or yielding to a guru is?

A - Same as Christ idol. Same as Catholicism. Same as any religion, as it were. It is not bad. It is not negative to learn from others no matter what form they take. Yet, it is bad to let another take on your own understanding, your own growth process. This is not of the Light and this should not be a consideration in something that you feel is a growing thing.

Q – Could you please explain the White Brotherhood?

A – I may say that there is a limited view of this concept. This is not only of a certain number. I feel there is a difference that is a false distinction at this time. For in spirit terms All in the Light is The White Brotherhood.

Q – How does the word wholeness apply to a human being, Janith?

A – Wholeness as in balancing? Balancing of soul, body, emotion, mind, and spirit takes wholeness, centeredness, God. None of these pieces may be "un" at ease with themselves or there will be no alignment. We are speaking of alignment.

Q – What is alignment?

A – Balance.

Q – What is Balance?

A – It is taking each piece and making them fit nicely together. Not one bigger, one smaller; not one lesser, not one greater. Putting them together to be one, as is the Universe.

Q – How can we best balance spirit and physicality while on earth?

A – I may say that balance usually occurs by pouring as much into one as into the other. It is as simple as this.

Q - **What is the Flame you refer to,** **Janith?**

A - *I may say that the Flame is of heart center, is of what is connected in soul body to the greatest I.   Flame is that of the place we wish to call love vibration.*

Q - **What is the purpose of meditation?**

A - *Meditation is a quieting time.   For human livings do not appear to give themselves space: time for them to be that heaven, to be that center, to be that balance.   And in order to obtain optimum growing knowledge from all lessons to be learned, we must come from a place of peace.*

Q - **Can we have some colors and their** **uses for meditation purposes?**

A - *I may begin with the highest healing color which is purple.   It is of a very spiritual nature.   In meditation it is a great caller for high spiritual guidance.*
     The next color may be that of blue. Only in spiritual matters, I may say. And if person is having difficulty with dealing in this color because of another meaning earth has put on it - such as sad, depressed - do not use.   Yet, I may say that if you may get past this, blue is a very healing color because it is calming, soothing, quieting.
     The third is that of yellow.   It signifies openness to healing.   I will say that yellow and green should be used in conjunction, for one is open or receptive, the other is active.

Q - Are there other ways to heighten soul awareness besides meditation?

A - Many.

Q - May I have some other examples?

A - Soul awareness is heightened through dreams, if that is recognized. It is only the intention of the recognition that must be focused on. For then any means may be used.

Q - Janith, what is the most efficient way to counteract Fear?

A - In a meditation, if a person would look into their centers and see which center is a fear center, it should materialize on soul body or in physical form. Then one should meditate and find out where love center is. And then, any time one sees the fear center, one should consciously switch to the love center. But this must be a conscious balance.

Q - If one listens to a tape recorded meditation rather than being in the direct presence of a spirit channeled healer, is it less effective?

A - I may say that many of the meditations are quite good, yet they are not as healing as coming directly from spirit on recorder or not. The best meditations are given by spirit channeled healers, for the vibration is already healing.

Q - Janith, what is centering and how should it be done?

A - Centering is a calling from heaven to be at peace as you once were and as you will be.   To be able to live on earth but not of earth.   How?   Each individual must find the way to get to that place of heaven within.

Q - Can you make a correlation, Janith, between God, The Light and centering?

A - Hmm.   The correlation is one of One. For being centered is finding God Light.

Q - Could you give a centering exercise?

A - In meditation, you may sit on the ground, drawing energy from earth, centering it within your perineal gland. This will help in your centering process, for going through many of the chakras does not center on the One: for many is then a different concept of the One. Just in your centering on a one, rather than the many, will help center.

Q - Should White Light be used for protection?

A - White Light protects from other planes.   Different colors must be used in meditation for different purposes.   That of green, that of anything that is strongly related to earth's growing process, can be used as a centering to ground or earth oneself.

Q - Janith, could you explain how we can tell the difference between spiritual emergence and psychosis?

A - I do not feel that trading one label for another is quite what we are about. For if we label one spiritual emergence, then all others become psychosis? Do we not miss the point of what we are asking?

Q - What we are really asking is, can the outcome of either spiritual emergence or psychosis be health?

A - Of course. Healing takes many different forms. We must not put judgements on how it looks.

Q - Should we begin to create Spiritual Emergency Networks?

A - Creating Spiritual Emergency Networks is quite important on all levels, in all spiritual situations, for there is so much fear at this time, in the beginning of communication, in the beginning of trying to come in contact with spirit. And, I may say, it could only help.

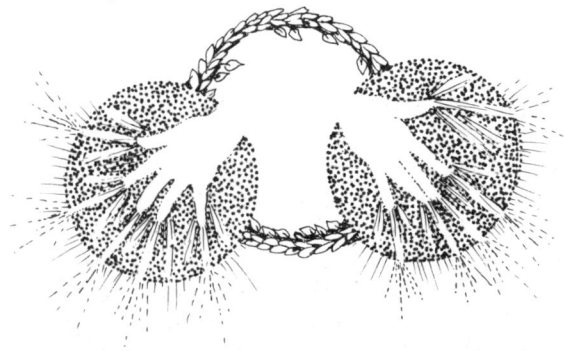

Q - **What is the basic responsibility** of a
spiritual counselor Janith?

A - Responsibility? The first
responsibility is to not feel
responsible. For truly we are not that
big in the universe. We are only
attributes. And others pick up for our
mistakes. So, I may say, that truly to
feel responsible is not to be a spiritual
counselor.

I may say that the <u>attributes,</u> the
<u>qualifications,</u> of spiritual counselor
could be seen as looking at a whole human
being in both "I's." And working with
both "I's" with whatever help one sees
fit to use.

Q - **In one of your answers you said**
"esseric" body. Did you mean etheric?

A - Esseric body is essence of man
living. Essentric body is essence of
senile man living (we are having fun.)
We mean esseric not etheric. Esseric is
essential. It is the essence of soul
body. It is soul knowledge.

Q - **Can that be touched by another or**
tampered with?

A - Of course. If allowed.

Q - How can we ground ourselves while on the spiritual path?

A - Grounding is a funny word. Earth yourself by being with the earth. Earth yourself by knowing your own center of the soul. For if you remain in touch with truth, your soul is always grounded (earthed). Have no fear of slipping into our plane mentally if you are strongly attached to earth. Each must do this in his/her way.

    The spiritual path is followed only when one is doing and walking along the route of one's plans once made. They go side by side. As long as you have one, you know you have the other.

Q - There are many people, Janith, who are caught up in ego, power, and arrogance. Why is this dangerous when one is on the spiritual path?

A - It is like mixing vinegar, oil, water ....and gas. It explodes when there is a light near it. I may say that ego and power are seducers. They are not of the Light, so if these become quite big on the spiritual path, then these ones are open to dangerous situations.

Q - On the spirit path, Janith, we are told to practice non-attachment and letting go. What is the purpose of this, and how can it be accomplished?

A - I may say that there is a faulty mechanism in this thought process. For one, if we must concentrate on letting go, we are not doing such. Non-attachment?

I feel there are some healthy attachments on the earth plane: parent - child, child-parent, grandparent- child, person - body etc. These are some attachments that need to be in a less restrictive way.

I feel that when one reaches the attainment goal of unconditional love vibration, then it automatically becomes non-attached giving, loving, letting go of fear, vibration.

Q - How can one practice non-attachment and still enjoy life to its fullest?

A - When we are living from a love vibration is the only time life is at its fullest.

Q - Is service enough of a path?

A - Nothing is <u>enough</u> of a path. <u>Nothing</u> is enough. More than is enough. Always past the point of comfort, that is enough.

Q - Is positive or negative visualization really as powerful as "they" say it is.

A - Positive thinking is one of the first steps in understanding that all are from the Light. Positive is a growth process, negative is not. Negative brings one to steps already taken, and postive takes one towards steps not taken yet. It is right. It is good, but not to make something happen. It is a good way of thought process. It is not the way to materialize wealth, happiness. It is a form of growth as long as it is in a thought-process sense.

Q - Can a human being heal himself/ herself by imaging? If not, what should be the basis of the new healing modality?

A - Anything is possible. Yet, I think the best course of action is to raise oneself to that higher positive thought process, which means that the healer, as it were, must live in that healing state at all times. It cannot be something that you can accomplish only in a sitting, only in a healing time of a day. It must be focused on as a thought process.

Once it is achieved (that you are living at that highest healing vibration) at any time a healing could occur, to anyone you meet. It does not need to be requested, for it is on that wave length, and will automatically appear.

Q - **Why does healing oneself seem so difficult?**

A - Because, rightly, it is difficult for ones in human form to achieve such a high positive thought process. Once that is known to be the mechanism that carries the vibrations to a healing power, then it is not quite as difficult as when one does not know where the vibration is or how it is affecting the healing itself.

Q - **Janith, could you explain what a miracle is?**

A - This is an important question. A miracle is the most beautiful recognition of a soul, of its higher spirit, in its communication with its higher spirit. It is bringing down some of that spirit into the physical through that soul. It remains to be the highest connection that people may be able to see, as it were, on earth, between that soul and spirit. It is the highest "I".

Q - **What do you feel about the Course in Miracles, Janith?**

A - I feel any course in miracles is wonderful.

Q - **Janith, how do you feel about out of body travel and uses?**

A - Ha! I am always out of body. So I must feel good with it. Uses? It is the only way I know to get around.

Q - Does the aura originate from within?

A - Always the point of origin is within. For it is personal color emanating from condition of soul body.

Q - What do you feel about aura cleansings, and how should they be done?

A - I may say that they are fine for physical ones as long as intention is one of releasing, of getting rid of, of letting go. And they should be done by high spiritual beings who have been in contact and are being guided by high spiritual forces. I may say as well that after aura cleansing, these "healers" must ask of high spirit to be cleansed as well.

Q - Janith, I know there are gifts that can be developed. Is aura reading a gift that can be developed and, if so, how would one go about learning it?

A - Most definitely these things can be learned, developed. Yet, they must begin with a completely open soul, open mind. I may say, the beginning is always internal cleansing. Once you are open to spirit, you may do any dance you wish.

Q - Janith, what is the magnetic field made up of, and is there another name for it?

A - We do not like magnetic field?

Q - I mean does it have a correlation?

A - Correlation? Aura. It is made up of quite a lot of energy forces - as well as positive ions and negative ions.

Q - Can you describe the chakras? What are they, and what do they do?

A - Chakras are very interesting ideas. They are energy centers within physical body. They do have little threads attaching themselves to soul body. Many things have been written about chakras; they are correct. The only thing that is not correct is that they do not encompass that soul body connection. That is quite important.

Q - What is chakra cleansing and is there a need for that?

A - Opening, opening, opening.

Q - How does one do that?

A - By opening.

Q - Is there a way for people to just leave the physical when it's time to die - some way for consciousness to just slip out the Crown chakra?

A - Of course, of course. Many of the masters have done this.

Q - Can you tell us what Kundalini energy is, and how you feel about spiritual practices which raise it?

A - Raising any kind of energy is quite beneficial to All, the One, God, The Light. Kundalini is fine. It is one way of instilling consciousness in a very fast-forward movement.

Q - Can you give us a definition of vibration?

A - Vibration of which I speak when I speak of magnetic field?

*Q - **What we wanted to know was, are people of different vibrations?***

A - Of course. This is why we use names and numbers to identify. It is by vibration. Also, emotions have different vibrations to them, considering that Fear is the lowest of vibrational energies and Love being the highest. Definition? Molecules of an energy source moving at a very fast motion would be high vibration. Moving slower would be a lower vibration.

*Q - **Are people with a higher vibration more evolved?***

A - Consciousness of high vibration is more evolved.

*Q - **Does laughter raise one's vibration?***

A - Of course.

Q - What effect does crying have on a vibration?

A - Crying in self-pity does not raise one's vibration. Yet, crying in releasing raises vibration in order to be able to laugh.

Q - How can one not allow one's own energy to mix with others' energy?

A - Oh, contain oneself.

Q - Is there an exercise or practice to do that or is it just the intent?

A - It is conscious intent of controlling, using one's energies to highest potential. For when they are being blocked, they spill.

Q - What is the role of the mystic in society?

A - The same as any other's role, to aid in the growth of All. The mystic is one of divine peace and should help others in their own findings of that peace. The mystics eyes are opened wider; therefore, they can see more so they can do more. But that is each and everyone's responsibility, to help others experience their own understanding of the Light, The One, The All-Knowledge. You are given eyes, you must see. You are given a mouth, you must speak. You are given ears, you must hear. You are given legs, you must walk. As long as one is really doing and utilizing all parts, the Whole will inevitably follow.

Q - What will psychics be used for in the NOW and future?

A - *Oh, I certainly hope they are not used. I feel their choices may be of higher development. I may also say they are a good beginning place. Different people are ready for different types, different forms, of spirit at different times.*

Q - Janith, what is the difference between psychic and spiritual?

A - *I may say that psychic seems to imply a knowing; spiritual seem to imply a seeking, a not knowing.*

Q - Can you tell us how you feel about Dowsing, Runes, and Tarot?

A - *I feel intention, vibration, and the way it is used is most important. For these can become traps.*

Q - Can you tell us, Janith, what you feel about the Cayce and Nostradamus predictions about disaster and the end of the world?

A - *I feel it always better to focus on positive manifestations. Why would we speak of disasters?*

Q - When a spirit dies, or goes on or is
incorporated does it then become part of
the entity God?

A - Everything is contained in what we
call God, yet, spirits do not transform
into the Ultimate of that reality until
all do.

Q - Can you give us three qualities that
a hopeful healer must have integrated
into personality, as well as soul, before
true work can be done on the physical
plane?

A - Of course.   Love vibration - which is
different from only love. Compassion yet
not pity.   And the third is of spirit
connection: "embodiment" if you wish to
call it that,   being quite evolved,
strong, yet balanced.

Q - Could you tell us what the Astral
plane is?

A - The astral plane is a very tricky
existence. Yet, I may say, one never has
to exist or see astral plane in order to
progress into higher planes or realms.

Q - Could you tell us who is in the
Astral plane that we consider dangerous,
if earthbound spirits are here on our
plane?

A - Very interesting question. The
astral plane is made up of all souls'
shadow sides.

Q - All souls above and below?

A - There are no souls above the Astral plane. What I am speaking of is all physical and earthbound souls. Their shadow side remains in the Astral plane.

Q - Do unresolved aspects of past lives remain in astral plane until each soul incorporates them?

A - Of course.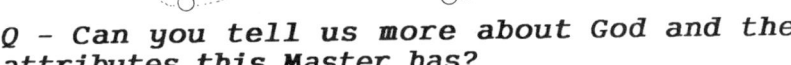

Q - Can you tell us more about God and the attributes this Master has?

A - To know ourselves is to know the attributes of God.

Q - Janith, can you comment on how one can become enlightened and still be enough of the earth plane to truly raise consciousness in the highest and best way possible?

A - I would suggest a formula of one quarter spirit, three quarters earth. I have always said earth is the best teacher. That is why you are there.

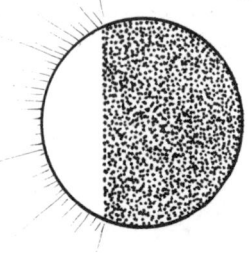

Q - What is the main purpose of enlightenment?

A - To attain higher understanding, to raise all consciousness off the earth plane, so it need not exist as it does anymore. This is to be our ultimate goal as holy ones.

Enlightenment is all about daily living here, there and everywhere. It means nothing else but to live each day as a master would. Treat earth and every human living as you yourself would like to be treated. Each day is a new experience toward eventual enlightenment. Each one has a chance at Nirvana, almost as a lottery. So pick the right numbers for your life and you shall win!

Q - Is there anything more you'd like to say? Any way we can help more to speed our consciousness toward its goal in any way?

A - There are many ways to do this. Of course, this is one. Communication with other planes remains the easiest, and in this case, the best, way to develop. Because any interaction between two beings, three beings, four beings...does not matter how many, gives different sights, different worlds, different visions, different thoughts. And in that interplay, different ideas of different realms.

Meditation inward. Meditation is very good, for it does put you in touch with other realms. This will always remain important because we have much to teach each other.

POSITION DURING MEDITATION:

Seated - with legs apart firmly
planted on ground, and both arms open
(whichever is comfortable - up to the
heavens or out to the wind) On
inhalation, arms must be open for centers
to be accepting and this is what this
affirmation is about. On exhalation,
drop arms down in front or on sides.

#1 - ACCEPTING CHANGE - LETTING GO

AFFIRMATION:

    I am of unconditional Love
    I am of unconditional Acceptance
    I breathe in acceptance
    I exhale rigidity

    I keep myself from learning,
    from growing, from God's gifts,
    when I do not accept
    what is given by Universal Consciousness.

                        REPEAT 3 TIMES

MOTION MEDITATION:

    Raise arms as we are breathing in
(through nose) the ability to let go.
    Drop arms as we are breathing out
(through mouth) the manifestation of
letting go. This should be done in the
same position as the Affirmation.

    Breathe in the ability to let go and
open acceptance (Raise arms)

    Breathe out the manifestation of the
letting go. (Drop arms)

  Please repeat 12 times slowly.

This position must be a little different for it will not be so releasing in its manner for it is something that is being done internally. Hands must be placed in open, hands on knees, palms upward position.

#2 - SWITCHING FROM FEAR VIBRATION TO LOVE VIBRATION:

AFFIRMATION:

I   AM LOVE; I HAVE BEEN BORN LOVE.
I   AM LIGHT; I HAVE BEEN BORN LIGHT.
I   AM GOD; I HAVE BEEN BORN GOD.

REPEAT 3 TIMES

MEDITATION:

Breathe deeply the color pink and know that is the Love vibration that is filling up our body through our palms, our nostrils, through our bones, our cells, our being.

Now exhale all that we know to be Fear. We are exhaling the color Red.

PLEASE DO 12 TIMES

As this is happening we must focus on our heart center which is our Love center and then focus on our navel chakra which is our Fear center. Visualize pink coming into Love center and red going out of navel center in a circular motion within our torso or centers until all the red is has turned to pink.

This will take a different amount of time for different people depending on the amount of Fear that needs to be changed into Love vibration.

#3 - PRAYER FOR CHILD AT BEDTIME

I am an innocent being of Love. I have come to this planet to help change consciousness. Through evolution I will learn, I will grow, I will become one with God, The Light. I bless all those who are trying to attain such a goal, for we are all One. And as I sleep, and my consciousness enters the angel realm, I wish to send healings, to all who I know and love, from this angel plane. I will return in the morning with the Sun. For truly, I have been born of God.

AFFIRMATIONS TO BE USED BEFORE DOING ANY
MEDITATION:

To raise vibration:

    I AM LIGHT; I AM LOVE;
    I AM LOVE;   I AM GOD;
    I AM ONE;   I AM LOVE.

Repeat for as many times as you must to
feel the difference.

For TRUST:

    I trust the Universe will give me
what I need.
    For I have released all wants and
expectations,
    And am open to anything the Universe
will provide for my highest growth,
     Given out of Love, by God, at this
time.

                    REPEAT 3 TIMES

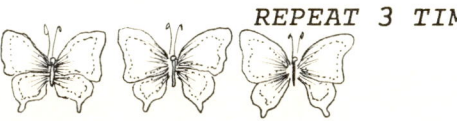

PROTECTION:

    I   AM OF LIGHT
    I   AM OF GOD
    I AM SEALED AND PROTECTED BY
    THE WHITE LIGHT OF LOVE

    I HAVE NO FEAR, SO IT HAS NO CONTROL

    I AM OF LOVE,
    I AM OF GOD,
    I AM OF LIGHT.

THE LIGHT

*"To know ourselves
is to know the attributes
of God."*

JANITH

"We, in the Light, live in a very peaceful, very loving way that all on earth have tried to accomplish in different forms, in different ways, in different lifestyles. Yet, if we release the trying, if we release the wanting, then we will be in eternal peace. For that is what we are. We are of Light. So look inside to your flame, find your Light and you will truly be one with God, The One, The All Knowledge.

Blessings,

Janith

Q - Who is God?

A - God is the master of all masters. At the beginning twelve masters were spoken of. God is the anonymous thirteenth. Yes, that is why it has become an important number. God is the most unknown to the human plane therefore the most feared. So springs up a negative tone to the thirteenth, as in Friday.

He/She is the most divine of all beings, an overseer of all planes, past sage, past wise person, past all.

218

Q - What is the Light?

A - The Light is the clue that God is there within. The Light is a relation to the higher level of the astral planes. The Light becomes a symbol of protection for human livings because of its connection with God. It's too hard for the human mind to abstract with nothing to symbolize a meaning.

Q - Is All only the Core Group or does it consist of other levels as well?

A - I may say that when we speak of All it is different from when we speak of All - Knowledge. When we speak of All, it includes all. I may say that when we speak of All - Knowledge, it is mostly I speak of, as you would like to say, the Core Group of Twelve Healers and of The Thirteenth Master.

Q - Are you from God?

A - Yes, I am from God, The Light, The All Knowledge.

Q - Where do you live?

A - We reside in the Light. As you have houses, we have our space. We each are on different levels of the spiritual plane yet the Light encompasses all.

Q - Why would a spirit choose not to incarnate?

A - Ah, you have a question that has been with <u>me</u> for a long time. I enjoy where I am. I see the limitations of body, I see the limitations of mind yet I am interested in these things. I am not willing to make that choice yet. Maybe one day, as in your earth talk, I will decide to join the human race. Yet, this may not be a progression for me. I do not know at this time, I do not know at the point I am at. I am not needed as a physical body right now, and I do not need from physical body now. So there is no growth process which would be accomplished at this time.

Q - Are there celebrations on your plane or special markers to indicate success, learning or growth?

A - Celebrations? Celestial celebrations come forward with growth, but it is not the same as concept of celebration that human livings have. It is quite different a concept for in knowing we have taken another step toward the Light, we, in and of ourselves, which becomes All, the Universe, the One, celebrate. For it does not need to be a marked thing. It is known when that growth process takes its next step and then all are happy, all are right.

Q - What can be used as another name for God?

A - Renoman, Kawantaw, Yaweh, All Mighty, Great White Spirit, Highest Lit One, Enlightened One of the Deepest Kind, The Thirteenth Master. Pure White Love. Any of these will suffice, yet three letters, God, is easiest.

Q - What happens at the end of a spirit lifetime?

A - There is no end until the last person on earth, on other planets, in other consciousness reaches the same goal, the same level of consciousness.

Q - What is a spirit birthday?

A - Each step in the growth of that spirit remains a birthday.

Q - When was the beginning of all worlds?

A - How do you wish for me to put that in words you would be able to understand? There are storytellers in our world. I was not there at the beginning as it were for I am told that the beginning was too long ago for any to remember.

A beginning of a circle is hard to detect. There are few who were there at the beginning, and as I discussed of the Thirteenth master, He/She was the first that any of us could remember.

Q - If you don't remember the beginning and no new spirits are created, when and how did you come into being?

A - I had been formed closer to the beginning than most.

The way we're formed? The Thirteenth Master has the ability to create from start any being that He chooses to. I use He in the future for it is easier than constantly reminding of the androgynous nature of everything but human livings.

Q - If spirit has no soul then spirit is formed as well?

A - Spirit takes form, yes, once the Thirteenth has made a process that is sort of like a decision but not as formulated.

Q - Is the Thirteenth Master also spirit?

A - He/She is spirit in that He formulates spirit so that becomes an aspect of the Self that He considers Himself to be. Yet, He is different in makeup than we as spirits are.

Q - Is there a specific plane that you occupy most of the time?

A - I don't know whose time. Most of the time? I reside in the Light and I have been on the plane that is closest to Nirvana for quite a long time. Forever, as it were. I don't remember, or hear tell, of being anywhere else. That place is everywhere. I don't occupy one specific place as do human livings on earth. Earth seems to be a specific place because of their own concept of what reality is. My concept of my reality is of Oneness. And I am seemingly everywhere.

Q - **What do angels do for fun?**

A - We are always having quite good times.

Q - **Are there angel vacations Janith?**

A - That is to imply that angels have work. All is vacation when all is Love.

Q - Could you please tell us Janith about the average day in the life of an angel?

A - Quite funny. The average day? An angel does not have an average day. It is quite more than average. And quite more beautiful than beautiful.

TERI GRISWOLD is a mystic, and a spiritual counselor as well as a channel for JANITH. She and her husband Gordon have two children and live on Long Island.

TERI and JANITH are available for lectures, interviews, workshops and private appointments. You may contact them at:

STAR WATER
(The Center for Self-Discovery)
104 Park Avenue
Babylon, 11702, L.I.
(516) 587 - 8877

TO ORDER:

For additional copies of ON WINGS OF TRUTH please send check or money order for $12.95 plus shipping and handling charges to:

STAR WATER PRESS LTD.
104 Park Avenue
Babylon, 11702, L.I.
(516) 422 - 0008

Affirmation Cards also available.